HORSE CARE
FROM A TO Z

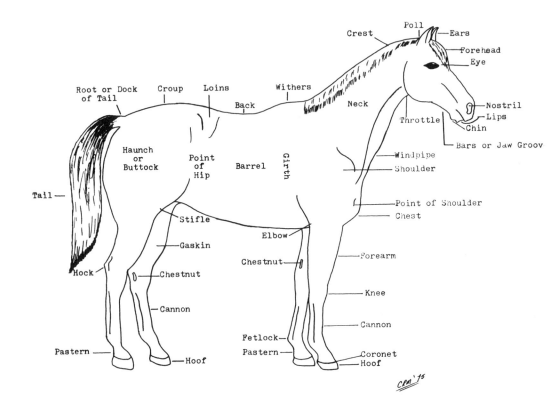

HORSE CARE FROM A TO Z

Carol R. Melcher

SOUTH BRUNSWICK AND NEW YORK: A. S. BARNES AND COMPANY
LONDON: THOMAS YOSELOFF LTD

A. S. Barnes and Co., Inc.
Cranbury, New Jersey 08512

Thomas Yoseloff Ltd
108 New Bond Street
London W1Y OQX, England

Library of Congress Cataloging in Publication Data

Melcher, Carol R
    Horse care from A-Z.

    Includes index.
   1. Horses. I. Title.
SF285.3M44   636.1   75-20599
ISBN 0-498-01691-9

PRINTED IN THE UNITED STATES OF AMERICA

CONTENTS

FOREWORD

An old adage says that the outside of a horse is good for the inside of a man. If so, it is because man, from ignorance rather than aestheticism, has always tended to judge and appreciate a thing only for its external appearance and beauty. But, I hope this book will be a large step in giving the average horseman some awareness and appreciation of the complexities of the internal workings of a horse and will allow him to use this new awareness in his consideration of proper husbandry.

A horse is not just one large animate object covered by horsehide. It is a multiplicity of organs and systems working together in a dynamic relationship to form a functional organism. All of the individual parts and systems must be taken into account for the proper care of the horse. In this respect, a horse is somewhat like an automobile, in that, periodically, all parts must be checked or at least visually examined to insure the proper function of the entire machine. Like an auto, there are aspects of a horse that should be frequently observed or checked by the owner. More complex and frequent checks of parts and functions of an automobile less familiar to the owner should be made as necessary by an auto mechanic. So it is with a horse. The owner should be familiar with everyday care and frequent problems that he may encounter. If he suspects a problem that cannot easily be determined or corrected, he will at least have taken the initiative in recognizing that there is indeed some sort of problem. He therefore can seek help, from a veterinarian or farrier, to further discern and correct the problem.

As an acquaintance of Miss Melcher, I can attest to her accomplishment as a horsewoman and to her capability to draw from her experience and knowledge in putting together the pages of this book. The book is a step in making the outside and inside of a horse good for the inside of a man, by giving the reader an understanding and appreciation for the entire horse in his consideration of everyday care.

Jim Koller, DVM

PREFACE

The horse and man have been together for centuries. The horse has been man's friend, his vehicle, his working machine, and occasionally, his food. The horse has been praised, glorified, and exhalted; and he has been hunted, starved, and ridiculed throughout his association with man. The horse has been given eloquent names in praise of his courage in battle, his speed on the track, his beauty of form; and he has been degraded with words like "crow-bait, skin, nag," and worse, when his form, manner, or temperament is less than perfect.

Down through time man has, between his outbursts of praise and scorn, attempted to find new and better ways of making his companion in work and pleasure more comfortable, better fed and housed, and has sought to erradicate many of the the diseases that plague the horse. Even so, there are still far too many horses that are not being kept properly, some from ignorance, and some from plain carelessness and lack of concern for the animal's comfort and well-being.

In nature, a horse will eat when he is hungry, will drink when thirsty, will find shade when he is hot, and sun when he is cold. He will lie down when it suits him and will stand when it suits him. His coat will thicken with the winter and will thin in summer. Most horses in the wild (and there are still a few of them) are thin, but hard of muscle and strong of wind. They live according to nature. The strong survive and the weak die, and though this sounds severe, it is really the only way that nature can assure the continuation of a species. If the weak and sick were allowed to live and breed and produce more weak and sick animals, the species as a whole would soon pass away. However, when man intervenes and domesticates any species of animal the weak and sick are cared for, and often made whole again, thus, changing nature. The animal must then learn to adapt to new, and oftentimes, foreign ways of living.

9

In our modern horse-keeping, the horse is oftentimes not allowed out on pasture, his feet may be required to grow to special lengths and shapes for showing, his coat is often protected year-round with blankets, he is fed special foods, and is kept within the strict confines of a stall and stable schedule. While this in itself does not constitute a problem, it does mean that the horse must have close attention to his physical care and well-being, as well as to his mental attitude. A high-strung horse can easily become bored and develop vices which, if they were to manifest themselves in a human being, would be called neuroses. Horses have quirks of temperament, eccentricities, and likes and dislikes, just as humans do, and it is only lately that the importance of a horse's good mental attitude has come to the horse owner's attention. Usually, if a horse is happy he will be mentally healthy, and if he is well cared for he will be happy. It is just about as simple as that.

Good horse care does not happen by accident. It is a thing that must be worked upon to achieve good results. Good horse care comes from knowing how to select the best types of feeds for your horse, what bedding to use to make him the most comfortable and to keep down odors and insect pests. It is knowing when and how to groom and trim the animal—even giving him a bath when necessary. Good horse care includes daily exercise, regular worming and shoeing. It also includes care of the animal's tack, his grooming kit, blankets and other stable equipment. Good horse care means doing for your horse before you do for yourself. It may mean staying up all night with him when he is ill or injured. Spending long hours walking after a hard ride to make sure that the horse is properly dried and cooled off. It means patience when the horse does not understand something that you are trying to teach him. It is hard work, mucking out stalls, carrying water if your barn is not equipped with plumbing, and keeping the stable area clean and safe. However, it is not all sacrifice. There is pleasure in having a well-trained horse that behaves on a trail ride — a horse that shines with health and vigor. There is much pleasure in knowing that your horse won a show ribbon because he is well cared for and performed at peak precision in his class. There is pleasure, too, in knowing that the work you are doing each day is bringing comfort and physical well-being to an animal that you undoubtedly have great affection for. After all, if you did not love horses you would not own one, would you? And if you own one you surely want to care for him in the best ways possible. Do you not?

Horse care, good horse care, is something that every conscientious horse owner tries his best to achieve for his horses.

ACKNOWLEDGMENTS

The author wishes to thank the following people and stables for their assistance in making this book possible.

Dr. James Koller DVM, Oley Valley Animal Clinic, Oley, Pa.
Mrs. Howard Paddock, "Northhill Farm," R.D. 1, Oley, Pa.
Mr. & Mrs. Richard DeLong, "Long D Ranch," Reinholds, Pa.
Miss Priscilla Moser, Wyomissing Park, Reading, Pa.
Mr. Glen Geesaman, Vinemeont Rd., R.D. 1, Reinholds, Pa.
F.M. Brown Sons Feed Mill, Sinking Springs, Pa.
Mr. Richard T. Curtin, "Furnace Hill Stable" R.D. 1 Fleetwood, Pa.

And special thanks to Mrs. Thomas Melcher, who provided much of the physical labor involved in the production of this work.

HORSE CARE
FROM A TO Z

1
ILLNESS AND AILMENTS

Everyone who owns a horse should know something about the care of his animal should the animal become sick or disabled for any reason. The horse owner should also know how to spot the more common illnesses and ailments that can overtake his horse. Many ailments are minor, but if untreated in their early stages, can become chronic when not recognized by the owner or groom in time. It is, therefore, a good idea to learn how to spot various illnesses and injuries so that you will have every opportunity for early treatment for your horse. Some of these injuries and ailments can be treated quite simply, while others may need the qualified attention of a veterinarian. However, early detection of both injury and ailments will make treatment easier, both for you or for the vet, and certainly for the horse.

BOWED TENDON — The bowed tendon is caused by a severe strain or sprain. The tendon of the leg bows outward, away from the bone, in a bowlike shape. In slight cases, the tendon may straighten itself and go back to its original shape and position. In severe cases, however, it will not cure itself, and the bow shape may be permanent. The leg is usually filled or swollen and hot to the touch. The horse will be very lame and will often refuse to be led or moved about in any way that will cause it to put weight on the injured leg. Apply cold compresses as soon as the bow is discovered, then call for the veterinarian.

15

BROKEN KNEES—This is an injury where the horse has fallen and has split open the skin of his knees. This type of injury may be mild or severe, depending upon how hard he has fallen on his knees, and upon what type of ground. The injury should be washed out with warm water, being sure that all foreign matter is removed (stones, gravel, dirt, etc.), then the vet should be called. Proper treatment by professional veterinarians may cure the injury and leave no scars. Home remedies may make the condition worse and, in most cases, the hair will grow in white, leaving a definite scar or line on the knees.

CAPPED ELBOW — (Also called *shoe boil*) The capped elbow is caused by a shoe on a hind hoof bumping against the elbow of the front leg when the horse is lying down. The elbow is bruised by the contact with the hind shoe and it will be swollen and oftentimes hot. Apply hot epsom saltwater for several days. The boil should either subside by itself, or it should come to a head, burst open, and drain. In most cases, the boil discharges pus for a number of days. This discharging matter should not be allowed to drain directly onto the skin of the leg below, as it may set up another infection should the animal have a break in the skin below the boil. To prevent this, coat the hair below the boil with a light film of mineral oil or petroleum jelly. The area around the boil should be carefully cleaned each day of any matter that may have drained down and dried there during the night. The boil itself should be checked as well, to ensure that it has remained open and is draining completely. When cleaning the matter from the leg, be sure to do so thoroughly. The best way is to use a piece of surgical cotton and warm water. If the boil will not open and does not go down after repeated hot applications, call the vet and he will lance it for you. **DO NOT** attempt to lance the boil or open it yourself if it does not open on its own. The chance of driving the infection deeper into the flesh and bone is great at this point, and amateur lancing will only increase that risk.

During the time of treament, the horse must wear a device known as a shoe boil boot. This is a soft padded cuff that is worn around the fetlock joint of the hoof that did the damage. This cuff keeps the hoof from bumping the sore elbow again, and thus, injuring it further. The vet will advise what futher care is needed.

CAPPED HOCK — This is a large swelling over the hock joint often caused by a sudden blow, or from striking against the wall of the stall while kicking. The joint of the hock is filled with fluid and may cause lameness, though not in all cases. Call the vet. He will inject the joint with a steroid to reduce the pain and swelling, and will give you further instructions for the horse's care. The usual treatment is to soak the joint with ice water for twenty minutes and then rub it with liniment for another twenty minutes, twice a day. Try it, if you cannot get a vet.

COLIC (Flatulent)— Colic is a stomachache caused by a buildup of gas in the horse's digestive tract. Flatulent colic causes continuous pain. The belly of the horse is filled with gas (flatulence), making the horse restless. He may lie down, then get up, then wander around, seeking relief from the discomfort. The gas is caused by food fermenting in the bowels, possibly from the horse being watered right after feeding.

Walk the horse and keep him warm. Also, give a colic drench. Ask your vet about one and keep his recipe on hand. Apply heat to the belly, such as heating pads, hot water bottles, hot blankets, etc., but be sure not to burn him. The application of heat is to relieve the pain and stimulate the action of the bowels. The sooner you can get the bowels working and the gas to pass, the sooner the horse will have relief. If this treatment does not work in three quarters of an hour, send for the vet.

COLIC (Spasmodic) — This is a more severe form of colic, with the pain coming and going in spasms. The pain is stabbing, rather than steady. The horse will sweat, roll, and may kick or bite itself. Use the same methods as above for relief, and above all, try to keep the horse from lying down and rolling. If the pressure in the bowel is too great and the horse rolls, the bowel may burst and cause death, or the pressure of the gas against the heart may stop it. Call for the vet in one-half hour if the pain is not relieved by the above treatment.

Colic is often caused by the horse eating moldy, wet hay, green hay or oats. It is caused by a sudden change in feed, as from mixed feed to oats, or vice versa, without the proper conditioning for the change. Too much green grass in spring, watering right after feeding instead of before, and working hard right after feeding are just some of the many causes of colic.

CONSTIPATION — Often this condition is called bowel impactions because that is exactly what happens. The stools pack in the bowels and cause a blockage. This condition is sometimes caused by worms, watering right after feeding that causes grain and feed to pack down, and sometimes old age, as the digestive processes slow down and become inadequate. Lack of water may also contribute to this problem.

The condition may sometimes be just a temporary cessation or halting of the bowels and may seem to be colic. Call the vet. Hot bran mashes may help, if the horse will eat. Many times an impacted horse will not eat because of the discomfort caused by the pressure in his bowels. Alfalfa hay may be fed, too, as it is a laxative. Be careful, however, not to give too much because it can cause gas.

Regardless of the cause, if the horse cannot pass his stools or appears to be straining to do so with little or no results, call the vet for help.

CRACKED HEELS — This condition is also known as *mud fever* and in advanced stages, *grease.* The skin of the backs of the pasterns cracks open, much like a severe case of chapping of the hands. The pasterns then scale over. The skin then splits open again, this time discharging pus, and then scales over again. If not stopped, the cycle will continue over and over again, getting worse each time and, in the end, may permanently cripple the horse. The best treatment is to soak the entire affected area in warm water, and when the scabs are soft, pick them off. Dry the hoof and leg with a napless towel, such as linen, pat-drying rather than rubbing, and apply cod liver oil or glycerin freely to the affected part of the leg. Keep the horse in his stall. The stall must be kept very clean and dry, and with this treatment, the feet should heal without any new scabs forming. If scabs form again, soak them and pick them off again and repeat the oil. Do not pasture or use a horse that has mud fever, for the condition is sometimes picked up or aggravated by properties in the soil — properties that will only lengthen the time taken to cure the condition. If allowed to go unchecked, the condition will cause the legs to become swollen and difficult to bend, the bending causing the horse great discomfort. In advanced stages, the matter that seeps from the raw areas will be very foul-smelling and the raw areas will take on a bright purplish red color. Granular lumps may appear as the scabs form and this condition is called *grapeing.* If mud fever or grease is suspected, all the fetlock hair should at once be removed, as this holds moisture. Many horses whose legs are washed and *not dried thoroughly* after use, acquire this condition.

If the condition does not clear up by the second removal of the scabs, do not wait for further steps, but call the vet, for medication is needed to affect a cure.

CRIBBING — This is more of a vice than a disease, however, it is so common that every horse owner should be aware of it and its treatment. This is simply a case of the horse chewing on any wood that he can get his teeth over. As he chews, he injests air, thus setting up the perfect situation for a colic attack. Another term for cribbing is *wind sucking*, and many horses injest so much air while pursuing this pastime, that their stomachs blow up way out of proportion and become quite hard to the touch.

To stop this habit, for it is mainly done through habit, though it may be started by a salt or vitamin deficiency, get a cribbing strap. The cribbing strap is a leather strap approximately two inches wide that is buckled around the horse's neck, just in back of the ear. The strap stops the horse from flexing his neck enough to permit him to get his teeth over his favorite chewing spot, usually a fence, a post, or the side of his stall. Some cribbing straps are designed with a pressure attachment and sharply pointed short, spikelike prods. When the horse holds his head in its natural position, the collar is just a smooth strap around his neck, however, when he flexes his neck to crib, the muscles of his neck press upward against the attachment and he is pricked by the prods. While this sounds much worse than it actually is, it does have its disadvantages. If used for a prolonged period of time it may teach the horse not to flex his neck at all, and this can be a definite disadvantage when riding, particularly at the higher levels such as dressage, where flexing of the neck is required.

The cribbing strap does not interfere with the horse's ability to eat, drink, or graze, but it does stop him from cribbing. Another idea is to buy cribbing paint that is used to paint all of the wood in his stall. Cribbing paint leaves a coating on the wood that is very disagreeable to the taste, and even the worst cribbers think twice about chewing on wood that has been treated with this substance.

CURB — This is a severe strain of the tendons that run down the back of the hind legs, causing severe lameness. It is sometimes called *curby hock*, for the area around the hock is swollen. Do not try and treat this condition yourself. Call the vet.

DIARRHEA — This is a case of constantly runny stools. It may be caused by a variety of things such as bad feed, too much green grass, worms, etc. If the feed is the cause of the condition, change it, making sure that all of the bad feed is disposed of, preferably by burning. If grass is the cause, remove the horse from pasture until the condition corrects itself. If you suspect worms as the cause, take a stool sample to your vet for analysis. Diarrhea is very debilitating and will quickly run down a horse's health. If changing the feed, or removal from pasture, or worms is not the answer, then call the vet as soon as possible.

ENCEPHALITIS — This is one of the worst of the equine diseases and is also known as *sleeping sickness*. Sometimes it is called *brain fever*, for it produces inflammation to the covering of the brain. It is caused by a mosquito-carried virus, though not all mosquitoes carry it. The mosquito bites an infected animal, incubates the disease in its own body, and then bites your horse. Encephalitis is most often fatal, but there are preventative serums available from your veterinarian. Ask your own vet about innoculations. They may save your horse's life.

FISTULA — A fistula is a deep-seated, pocketlike infection, usually found on the poll or withers of the horse. Often it is caused by a heavy rubbing pressure (such as a poorly fitted saddle that rubs the withers), or as a result of a severe blow. The fistula on top of the head at the poll is often called *poll evil*, and may often be located where the bridle will come in contact with it when worn. A fistula is really a very bad boil, and they are hard to cure because of their location, such as on the top of the head, on the withers, or between the shoulder blades. Being on top of the head and between the shoulders they cannot drain to the outside, so they often drain downwards under the skin, infecting healthy tissue.

Hot compresses should be applied as soon as the fistula is noticed and continued until it opens (1—2 days.) After the wound is opened, and if it drains out, it should close within two days. If not, call the vet. Fistulas, in the long run, are best treated by a vet.

Never ride a horse with a fistula. The saddle will rub or press on withers fistula, and the bridle will press on a poll fistula. By riding, you will only drive the infection deeper.

GALLS — Another name for galls is *saddle sores*, mainly because most galls are caused by ill-fitting tack that rubs open spots on the horse. A drying ointment, such as blueing, is to be applied to the affected area and the horse should not be ridden until the sore is healed. If rubbing persists and is not treated, a fistula may result. (See above)

GLANDERS — Although this disease has almost been eradicated in this country, it still bears mention, as it was once a major killer of horses, and with today's mass transportation, most parts of the world with its diseases, are mere hours away. Glanders is a contagious disease that affects mucous membranes in equines. The disease is fatal to the horse in most cases amd can be transmitted to man. The mucous membranes in the nostrils and lungs develop abcesses, as do the glands in the jaw groove. Abcesses are lumpy, running sores. If the horse is to be saved, immediate medical care is a must. If the abcesses appear on the outside of the body, such as on the underside of the jaw, the disease is known as *farcy* and the abcess is known as a *farcy bud*. There are preventative innoculations available to prevent this disease.

HEAVES — This condition is also known as *broken wind*. It is a condition where the vesicles or small pockets in the lungs are broken down or in a deteriorated state. In the early stages, the horse has a hard, sharp, phlegmless cough, heard most frequently at the beginning of a ride, and the horse may rock slightly back and forth when breathing. Breathing in the later stages is labored and sometimes noisy and thick-sounding. As the disease progresses, the breathing becomes marked and the rocking more noticeable. This is because the horse inhales once and exhales twice in the same breath. This is done because he cannot expel all of the inhaled breath on the first try. Also, a muscular ridge develops along the loin, just behind the last rib. This is caused by the exertion of muscle during exhalation and it is called the heave line. The rocking motion is backward when he inhales and forward twice as he exhales. In bad cases, you not only can feel him rock when you are mounted, but the motion can be plainly seen.

Heaves are often caused by running a horse past his endurance. He gasps and gasps for air until the small vesicles of the lung rupture. They do not repair themselves, nor can they be repaired. By wetting or dampening all of the horse's feed and keeping his barn as dust free as possible, also by feeding special feeds available at your feed dealer just for "heavey" horses, you may alleviate his symptoms, but he will never be good for hard or fast work again. Consult your vet for treatment and try and catch it early, even if you just suspect heaves.

INFLUENZA — This is exactly the same in horses as it is in man. It is an upper respiratory infection. Call a vet and do not attempt to cure it alone. Neglect of influenza may lead to heaves, or the horse may strangle on his own mucous discharges. The symptoms are the same as in man. The horse will have chills and fever, a sore throat and runny nose, and may have bouts of sweating. Horses with sore throats will not eat and many will not drink. Get your vet as soon as possible, before the mucous has a chance to thicken and build up in the animal's lungs.

LAMINITIS (Also called Founder) — This is one of the most painful of all horse ailments. Founder is caused by a variety of things. Too much food, food that is too heating, working too hard when the horse is out of condition, and watering when hot. Also, feeding spoiled or bad feed, allowing the horse to stand when hot, running him on rock hard ground or macadam for long periods of time, will all cause founder if the conditions are right.

The process of founder is a bit complicated. The tissues inside the hoof become inflamed and swell up. These are the *laminae* of the hoof, wherefrom the disease derives its true name; Laminitis or inflammation of the laminae. The laminae are interlocking meshes of tissue that swell and become gorged with blood, and since the foot or hoof cannot expand to permit the swelling, the mesh breaks down under the strain and causes great pain. Oftentimes the bones inside the hoof, which are supported and held in position by the laminae, drop down towards the sole of the hoof as the membranes give way. This often pushes the sole of the hoof downward and causes flat feet or permanent crippling.

The hoofs are extremely hot to the touch, and the horse is in severe pain. If he walks at all, he will most likely support his weight on his hindquarters and hop forward so that he puts as little weight on his sore front feet as possible. Founder affects only the front feet in ninety-nine cases out of a hundred. Many times the horse will lie down and refuse to get up. He may also stand in the stall and grunt or breath hard, and sweat in patches as he would do when colicky.

As soon as founder is suspected, call the vet. He can administer a pain killer and an anti-inflammatory drug that will reduce the swelling. Have the shoes removed as gently and as quickly as possible, as their weight and pull on the hoofs will only make the condition worse. Withhold all feed until the vet arrives. He will instruct you on feeding procedures.

If you cannot get a vet, withhold all feed for twenty-four hours. The horse may have as much water as he likes. Usually the horse will drink much water because of the fever in his feet. Be sure, however, that the water is not cold.

Soak the feet in cold water for twenty minutes every two hours for the first day, every four hours the second to fifth days, then, three times a day for the next two weeks.

After the first twenty-four hours have passed, you may begin to feed, but you must be very careful. I have found through experience, that a good feed of the following mixture and amount works well. Feed one-quarter the amount of his usual ration. One-fourth of this one-fourth is oats, while the other three-quarters of the ration is bran. (The first two feedings after the twenty-four hour fast should be bran only). The one-fourth ration of the above mix should be fed for the first week. Never use a mixed feed after a horse has been foundered, even when he is better, because of the heating and fattening properties it contains.

Your horse will lose weight on the above quarter ration diet, but you may save his life. The horse should have twice the normal amount of hay at each feeding so that he does not feel too empty, and also to keep him from swelling with air and getting colic. Also, he should have a vitamin supplement at each feeding to keep up his strength.

The second and third week, feed a bit less than half his normal ration. One-half of this half should be oats and the other half bran. Gradually increase the feed after the third week until he is back on his normal ration. **Slowly** cut down on the bran each day and increase the oats. By now, you should have been able to get a vet and he can instruct you further. Always use the vet's advice first. Ask the vet about riding the horse again. He will advise you as to what is best. If you are totally without a vet for some reason, do the following: Rest the horse for four weeks after the foundering. Do not ride him, lunge him, or work him for that time. Begin riding on the fifth week, but only at a walk for five minutes twice a day. Do this for the first week. Then you may **gradually** build up until the horse is working normally. Ride the horse on either grass, or other stoneless surface. Stones will hurt his feet and slow his recovery time.

Oftentimes after foundering, the hoofs become deformed and grow outward and curl up with large, wavy ridges running around them. Foundered feet always need special shoeing. Short toes, raised heels and resets every six weeks will be the usual procedure. Ask your vet when to reshoe after the initial attack of founder.

LAMPAS — Lampas is really neither an illness nor an injury, but is a condition that presents itself as a swollen, spongy lump on the roof of the mouth, usually just behind the front teeth. It usually interferes with the animal's feeding, as it makes the mouth so sore that it is painful for the horse to eat. You often see lampas in horses whose upper teeth overlap the lower ones, rather than butting together. This condition of the upper teeth overlapping the lower ones is called *Parrot Mouth*, due to the resemblance of a parrot's beak. The lower teeth, instead of engaging the uppers as they are supposed to do, slide behind them when the horse bites or chews, and bump against the gums behind the teeth. The constant bumping produces a sore spot that fills with blood and lymph. A laxative diet will sometimes cure lampas, particularly if it is in a young horse who is cutting his permanent teeth, however, most cases of lampas need to be lanced by a vet and medication given until the condition clears up. Again, make no attempt to lance the lump yourself as you may do more harm than good with your treatment. If you cannot get a vet right away, and the horse will not eat because of the soreness of his mouth, try him with warm bran mashes until the vet is able to treat him.

LARYNGITIS — Again, this is much the same in horses as it is in humans. Usually the horse is reluctant to swallow and will not eat because he has a very sore throat. He may also have a runny nose. A vet should be called immediately, as sometimes the air passages swell shut. The vet will prescribe food and methods of getting him to eat. Also, he will tell you how to care for him and he will give medication. If the vet is not immediately available, a vaporizer, or a large tub of steaming water, placed under the horses nose so that he can breath the warm, moist air, may help. Be careful, however, not to burn the animal.

MANGE — This is a parasitic disease that causes the skin to wrinkle or blister and the hair to fall out in patches. It is caused by a mite that may live on the skin or has burrowed beneath. If you suspect mange, call the vet. The horse with mange will rub on anything he nears, scratching himself raw in the process. Treat the condition as ordered by the vet and disinfect the stall. This is usually done by painting the whole stall with *creosote*. Mange is very contagious, so keep the horse separated from the other horses.

In one form, mange may affect the legs and tail of the horse. The other types affect the whole body. There are three types of mange: *Sarcoptic*, which is nearly impossible to get rid of; *Soroptic*, which is less stubborn and more common; *Symbiotic*, which affects the legs and tail, is fairly easy to cure, and is seldom seen.

In most cases, mange is usually first seen on the side of the neck, just at the edges of the mane, and on the insides of the hindquarters, just at the root of the tail. If left untreated, the disease will spread across the back and down the sides of the animal. The hair will begin to fall off, leaving the skin smooth or with a few, scattered, reddish pimples. However, as the disease progresses, the pimples develop into clumps, each pimple containing a mange parasite or *acarus*, and they produce a fluid making a scab that hardens on the horse's skin. If allowed to progress, raised furrows will appear that will lead from one clump of scabs to the next. These furrows are tunnels under the skin that have been made by the traveling acarus. In advanced stages, the horse becomes feverish, looses appetite and drops weight, due to the constant itching of his body. Professional veterinary treatment is the only certain cure for a horse with mange. All clothing and blankets used on the animal should either be burned, as the parasites tend to burrow into them, or washed thoroughly, soaked with turpentime, and allowed to dry before using again.

NAVICULAR DISEASE — This is also known as *naviculararthritis*. Many horses with narrow heels and very high soles seem prone to this disease. Horses with very cupped soles tend to develop navicular disease because, in many cases, the frogs of their feet do not touch the ground as they should, and therefore, there is little or no shock absorption for the foot. The foot is in a constant state of being bruised and battered at each step, and this may result in an inflammation of the covering of the navicular bone or the tendon that passes over it.

The first symptoms of naviculararthritis is sudden lameness in one or both of the front hoofs, and pointing of the toes of the feet. Also, the horse may appear to be walking on his toes, which in reality, is exactly what he is doing. Most horses with navicular disease walk this way in order to keep any and all pressure off their heels. The soles of the feet of a horse with navicular disease will, in most cases, be very hard with little or no flexibilty, and many times the rest of the hoof will be the same. Horses with contracted heels also seem prone to this problem and it may be due to a decrease in the blood supply to the foot, owing to the contraction of the muscles, tendons, and blood vessels in the heels. Sometimes, this affliction is brought on by constant, hard or fast work on hard ground. One of the best treatments to alleviate the lameness in the early stages is to pull the shoes and have the heels trimmed down so that the frog of the hoof is made to touch the ground. While this may at first appear to make the condition worse, it will, in reality, place the frog in its proper position and begin to make it work in the shock absorption capacity that it should. By making the frog touch the ground, it will stimulate the nerves and blood vessels and aid in removing the inflammation. Working the horse in soft ground and pasturing him thusly, will help alleviate his problem, as will standing him daily in cold mud, thus lowering the inflammation temporarily. However, if allowed to progress, the disease may cause the tendons of the heel to adhere to the bone, or may cause the bone itself to ulcerate. When the foot reaches this stage there is very little chance of recovery and the animal may need to be destroyed. As the disease progresses, you will also notice that the hoofs become narrow, the horse may become pigeon-toed and the front of the pastern joint will develop a peculiar rounded shape, caused from the horse holding all of his weight on his toes for a continued period of time.

At the first signs or suspicion of navicular disease, call the vet.

OPTHALMIA — This is one of the most common causes of blindness or partial blindness in horses. It is caused by an infection behind the eyeball, and it leaves the eye covered by a bluish tinge. Sometimes this film is heavy and sometimes very light. Opthalmia usually starts with a running of the eye, sometimes caused by a plugged tear duct. Often the matter exuded from the eye will make the membranes of the eyelid swell, and the eye will look puffy and red, sometimes causing the lids to stick together. The eye should be bathed frequently with warm water, for if allowed to continue, the condition may become serious. The eyeball may become covered by a greenish cloudy film that will last for a few days. As this greenishness leaves, a small white spot will appear inside the eye. This may or may not disappear, depending on how severely affected the inside of the eye was by the infection, but wherever the white spot appears there will now be a blind spot. If the whole eyeball retains a bluish film, then total sight will be partially diminished.

Sometimes this disease is brought on by constant housing of the animal in a dark stable and bringing him outside into great brightness without allowing the eyes to first adjust to the change in lighting. Standing a horse in a very dirty stable where he is constantly in contact with strong ammonia fumes, may also start an opthalmic condition.

If opthalmia is suspected, call the vet at once. Also, keep the horse out of direct light, as this is a very painful disease or condition, and sharp light will aggravate it greatly.

PNEUMONIA — This is a disease that is common to both man and horse and may be passed from one to the other. As in man, pneumonia is caused by the *pneumococcus bacillus* and the symptoms are much the same. Pneumonia is an inflammation of the lungs, and in horses, it may follow influenza or a cold (as it may in man), or sometimes strangles, if they are not treated in time.

The horse will cough, shiver, run a fever, and he will have a runny nose. The matter from the nose may range from thin, slightly colored matter, to thick, deep yellow mucous. The horse's stools may also be coated with this matter and he will be constipated. The vet is a must, as the horse will need antibiotics. Untreated, pneumonia will kill. If it is not treated, and the horse somehow survives, he may very well have broken wind afterward. Most untreated diseases or colds of the chest and lungs will cause broken wind, due to thickening of the air passages left by the disease.

QUIDDING — Quidding is neither a disease nor an injury, but a condition that has been brought about by something else. A quid is a ball of hay or feed that the horse chews up in the normal fashion then spits out, rather than swallowing, most often because of badly worn teeth, abcessed tooth, or sore throat. If you find your horse quidding, call the vet.

QUITTOR — This is an infection inside the hoof and is often brought on by nail pricks, bruises of the sole of the foot, or other types of small puncture wounds. Since most wounds go unnoticed because of their lack of size, matter that has entered the foot by way of puncture has a chance to set up an infection. This infection inside the hoof procedes to produce sinus-like cavities in the delicate membranes on the inner hoof. Lameness then results, and sometimes drainage from one or more openings that may appear in the sole, or around the wall of the hoof. The matter will be dark in color and offensive-smelling. A vet is a must for a cure.

RINGBONE — Ringbone is a bony callosity or deposit of bone (calcium) that forms a hard, circular ridge, just above the hoof on the pastern of the horse. It causes lameness which, in the early stages, may disappear when the horse is worked, and may reappear after he has stood quietly for a while. It is caused by an irritation to the bone, possibly from a blow or bruise. It cannot be cured, only slowed down by a process called *blistering*. Ask your vet about this treatment. Blistering is done in the hope that a new injury or irritation that is caused by the blistering, will cause the old injury to heal along with it. Blistering also promotes heat and increases circulation to the area. However, though it may temporarily alleviate the problem, it cannot totally cure it. The horse will, eventually, have to be destroyed.

RINGWORM — Despite its name, this is not caused by a worm at all, but rather by a fungus infection of the skin. It usually starts with a cluster of small, water-filled blisters, much like poison ivy. However, as the center of the cluster of blisters begins to scab over, a new ring of blisters breaks out around it. This causes an ever-widening patch of raw skin in a circular pattern, thus, the name. This is a highly contagious disease, both in animal and man, and it spreads rapidly. The hair of the horse will fall out and skin will be bald, raw and weepy. Your vet will prescribe an ointment or lotion for this condition. Though it is not too difficult to cure, it does need a vet's attention. It will not heal or go away by itself.

ROARING — This is a condition associated with broken wind and often follows strangles. It is caused by atrophy or shrinking of the windpipe. When air passes to the lungs during inhalation, a roaring sound is produced. Though not painful, a roarer will usually not be acceptable for showing except in jumping classes, though he may be otherwise servicably sound. This condition is not curable. Usually the condition causes no problems, other than the possibility that it may cut down on the horse's stamina to some degree, as the windpipe cannot expand as far as it normally would under strenuous conditions, such as hunting or racing.

SAND CRACK — Due to dryness, the hoof often cracks when under stress. This condition is sometimes serious if the crack penetrates the horn of the hoof and causes lameness. The condition is minor if no lameness occurs and the crack does not penetrate into the quick or live portion of the hoof. It is vital to get moisture into the hoof and not to use the horse until the crack has grown out. A metal plate may be attached to the hoof, spanning the crack, to give support and halt progression of the crack. If the crack occurs at the top of the hoof, at the coronet, as often happens, a vet is a must to halt further damage. If the crack extends into the coronet area, the hoof may always carry a permanent scar, marking where the crack damaged the coronet tissue.

SHIPPING FEVER — This is a contagious disease that is akin to distemper in other animals. It is usually picked up in shipping a horse from one part of the country to another, hence, its name. It is usually passed from one infected horse to another through use of a single bucket for watering them all. It is also passed through one horse coughing, sneezing, or breathing on another horse in a confined space, such as railroad cars or any mass animal-hauling vehicle.

Horses with shipping fever cough, have a runny nose, and refuse to eat. In severe cases, the discharge from the nose may plug the nostril almost completely and complications, such as pneumonia or strangles, may appear.

If your horse gets shipping fever, or if you buy a horse that has shipping fever, get the vet at once. The horse must have medication, penicillin preferably, as shipping fever seems to respond best to that particular antibiotic.

As in any disease, the horse should be kept quite, out of drafts, and warm.

SHOE BOIL — See Capped Elbow.

SIDE BONES — This is a calcified ridge, much like ringbone, but on the side of the coronet of the hoof. The foot will be hot to the touch near and around the heels of the foot, and there will be a ridge that you can feel.

The most common causes of side bones are overwork on bad ground, and heredity. In some cases there will be no lameness if the condition is not too severe. If there is lameness, it goes away at rest, but returns as soon as the horse is used. It is best to get the vet. He will be able to treat it and possibly be able to tell you if it is going to get worse or not. Sometimes side bones can be halted with proper treatment. Also, the use of cushioned shoes may help by increasing the shock absorption quality of the foot, though the horse will never do hard work again.

SIT FASTS — These are hard, callousy lumps, usually on or near the spine, caused by poorly fitting saddles. Many sit fasts start as saddle sores or galls, but if left untreated, soon develop into a sit fast. The saddle rubs, sets up an irritation on the bone of the spine, and the irritated place fills up with calcium. Sometimes a sore or raw spot appears where that saddle has been rubbed. When the spot heals, it often leaves a lump, that may or may not get larger, and in many cases, when the scab comes off, all of the hair under it comes away as well. For some time after the sore has healed, the skin may flake off, much like dandruff, and it may be difficult to get hair to grow on the lump. (Try keeping the skin on the lump pliable with a little vaseline. This will also promote the regrowth of the hair.) Some sit fasts are painful, while others are not. In any event, once they are, they are there permanently, and any future saddle should have extra padding placed over the lump, or should not touch the lump at all. This is one reason to be sure that all of your equipment fits properly and never rubs.

SPAVIN — These are caused mainly by strains to the legs. The *bog* or *blood spavin* is a soft, puffy lump just below and inside the hock. The hock joint fills with blood or lymph and produces the lump. Bog spavins may or may not cause lameness and are usually caused by a strain or sprain of the hock joint itself. Begin treatment by applying cold compresses. Many tack shops sell chemical cold compresses for just such treatment. The cold in these plastic pouched compresses is produced by a chemical reaction and is retained for several hours. They may be placed directly on the sprained part and wrapped in place, and allowed to remain there until their coldness disipates. In most cases, bog spavins cause little trouble if treatment is begun at once. The horse should be confined, except for a very short walk on a lead, once a day until the spavin heals. Should there appear to be no progress in two days, call the vet. In most instances, regardless of treatment, the horse will have a permanent, spongy lump where the injury took place. The size of the lump will depend on the degree of injury done to the hock and the degree of good done by the treatment.

Bone spavin is a bony deposit on the hock which, when severe, may interfere with the movement of the hock joint. This needs a vet's attention, as do most horse ailments. Rest is one of the best cures, though pin-firing or blistering may also be required. After the lameness that is associated with bone spavin is gone, the hock joint will, in most cases, be enlarged and will remain so permanently.

A fairly uncommon spavin is the spavin of the knee. A hard lump forms on the inside of the knee that causes pain when the leg is bent upward. This spavin often appears along with broken knees, or if the horse bangs his knees severely in the stall, in a trailer, etc. This spavin is difficult to treat, due to its location and it is sometimes called an *occult spavin*; occult meaning hidden.

SPEEDY CUT — This occurs when the horse strikes the back of the front leg, usually just below the knee, with the toe of the hind foot. This is a form of overreach, and the cuts are sometimes deep and painful. If not too serious, that is, not appearing to require stitching, blueing may be applied after the area has been thoroughly washed clean. Blueing should be applied twice a day, and drying and healing should be noticeable by the second day. If not, call the vet. Speedy cut may also occur on the rear or the coronet, and if so, consult the vet for treatment as the coronet is a vital part of sound hoof growth.

STOCKING UP — This is a swelling of the legs during rest. Usually it is in the hind legs, and this too, is caused by overwork, usually when the horse is out of condition. The swelling usually goes down when the horse is worked and then the legs fill again after a night's rest. Rubbing the legs after work with a good brand of liniment most often helps, and walking the horse before and after work alleviates this condition. Walk the horse before working him to allow the blood in the legs time to circulate and warm up. Walk him after work to permit the blood to cool and slow down.

STRANGLES — This illness causes the glands in the horse's jaw groove to become infected or abcessed, often after the horse has had pneumonia or shipping fever. The glands swell and the horse has a fever, as he will have with almost any infection. If the abcessed glands do not open and drain, they should be lanced by a vet, who will also administer antibiotics to fight the infection. In severe cases, the glands will never completely subside, and they become thickened with scar tissue. Sometimes this can interfere with the proper flexing of the neck. It may also interfere with breathing. A horse with strangles will have difficulty in breathing too, when the condition is in effect. The mucous membranes of the nose and throat become so swollen, that the breathing passages are nearly shut. Early treatment is a must, for the passages may very well close completely if not treated. Fortunately, strangles are not too common.

STRINGHALT — Little is known about this affliction except that it seems to be a type of nervous disorder. It causes the horse to lift the hind legs extremely high in a jerky motion, as if he were a puppet on a "string." It does not, however, affect the horse in any way other than this peculiar walk, and the horse usually only walks this way when first brought out of the stall, prior to being warmed up for work. Confinement of the horse for long periods of time, not allowing him liberty to exercise at will, and using him very infrequently may all help to increase the chance for this ailment. Thus, there is the necessity of regular work, freedom, and roomy stall.

TETANUS — This is also called *lockjaw* for what it does in the advanced stages. In the horse, it is fatal once the symptoms appear. It is common to both animal and man, and the most common way to contract it is through open cuts, wounds, and punctures. The presence of the germ is common in most stable areas, as the bacteria lives in the soil. The presence of animal waste also appears to create favorable conditions for the bacterial growth. It is advisable for anyone who works with horses to have a tetanus shot regularly, and also to have his horse innoculated against it yearly.

Early symptoms in the horse are; extreme nervousness, jumpiness, and total oversensitivity.

If you even suspect tetanus, call the vet, for if you receive a cut while handling a tetanus infected horse, you may very well contract it from him, if you have not been immunized against it.

THOROUGHPIN — This is an ailment that is more unsightly than unhealthy. In most cases, it does not cause lameness, and does not affect the action of the horse. Thoroughpin is a small, puffed swelling on both sides of the hock, and most times, needs no attention or treatment of any kind. It is caused by a slight strain to the joint and is called thoroughpin because it appears to pass directly through the hock (Pinned through). If the area should appear to be sore, cold compresses applied for twenty minutes, three times a day for a day or two, should help.

THRUSH — This is a fungus infection of the frog of the foot and is usually, and most commonly caused, by the horse being kept in a wet, dirty stall. Some horses, however, may contract this disease no matter how clean their stalls are kept. They are simply prone to this type of bacteria or fungus, particularly those with deep frog clefts. This, however, is the exception to the rule.

The symptoms are; sloughing off of the outer layer of the frog, and foul-smelling hoofs. The skin that peels off is black, rubbery, and very offensive-smelling. A thin, oozing matter comes from the frog and is black in color, and becomes thicker as the disease progresses. In later stages, soreness of the frog, which may or may not cause lameness depending upon the animal, will become apparent.

If detected early, and if you check your horse's feet daily, you cannot help but notice it, it is one of the easiest things to cure. If you call the vet, he will usually allow you to stop at his office and pick up medication for this condition, or most tack shops carry a brand name product, just for the treatment of thrush. In the early stages, thrush can easily be treated at home with the proper medication.

TWISTED GUT — This is a fairly common ailment and happens most often when the horse has colic and tries to roll. In doing so, the horse may flip a loop of intestine over another, or turn the intestine so that when he gets up it knots. Twisted intestines do not permit passage of anything out of the bowels. There is severe pain and oftentimes the horse cannot stand up. Sometimes the horse will try to bite his sides. In other cases, if the horse remains on his feet, the hindquarters rock or sway as if the horse were going to collapse. Usually, the only cure is emergency surgery, and getting the vet as quickly as possible is a must if the horse is to be saved. If you have a horse with colic, try and keep him from rolling if at all possible.

WARBLES — These are more of a parasitic ailment than a disease. The warble fly, wherefrom it derives its name, lays its eggs under the skin of the horse. This may be anywhere on the body, but it is most common on the neck and saddle area. You can detect the eggs or larvae by the lumps they cause. The lumps are usually about the size of a quarter and fairly well raised and hard. They cause no discomfort unless under pressure, from a saddle for example, and will not cause trouble. They may be safely left alone if not irritated. If they come under pressure from the saddle, or if you wish them removed, then the vet should do it for you. Do not attempt to cut or squeeze them out yourself.

WEAVING — This may be considered either a vice or a nervous affliction, for it often appears in high-strung horses. When in the stall, the horse constantly swings his head back and forth in a rapid manner while swaying his body as well. Horses like this should be stabled where they can watch outside activity, or they should be outside as much as possible so that their attention is on something other than stall confinement.

The problem with horses like this, is that they fret themselves thin. It is difficult to keep proper weight on them, as the nervous condition burns it off. There is nothing medical to be done, only the stabling conditions suggested above, and if the horse is in strict, hard training, letting up on him for awhile may help.

WHISTLING — This is a condition somewhat like roaring, only the sound is a high whistle upon exhalation. It, too, is associated with damaged wind, but is not as severe as roaring. It cannot be cured, but usually causes no problems. Like roaring, it is just noisy, and may keep the horse from being shown in such classes as conformation, model class, etc.

WIND SUCKING — See Cribbing.

WORMS — There are a number of different types of worms that are common to horses and all of them are pests.

Strongyles — These are called round worms, and are the most common. They are round, white, and pencillike, and from four inches to ten inches long. These worms live in the digestive tract of the horse.

Ascaris — Also a type of round worm. They live in the lower intestine and rectum, and produce constant itching and tail-rubbing.

Blood Worms or *Red Worms* — These are two inches long and the most dangerous of horse worms. They live in the intestines, as do other types of worms, but if allowed to go unchecked, they will enter the horse's blood stream and attach themselves to the lining of the blood vessels, muscles, and other organs of the horse's body by small hooklike projections on their heads. They live on the horse's blood and are red in color.

Bots — Caused by the botfly or gadfly, bots are also quite common. These are picked up by ingesting the fly eggs that are laid on the hair of the horse's legs. They, too, live in the digestive tract.

Worms sap a horse's strength, make him listless and rob his coat of shine and luster. Symptoms of worms are as follows: Debility, feebleness, sluggish movements, emaciation, staring coat, hidebound, irregular appetite (sometimes none, sometimes ravenous), tucked up belly, badly digested feces, and tail-rubbing. Worming twice a year with a good commercial wormer, or a veterinarian-prepared wormer, is a must for healthy horses. I do not advocate tube worming, as it is very hard on most horses, and if the animal is debilitated by worms already, tubing may bring his condition even lower. Tubing is done by the vet, whereby, a tube is inserted into the stomach, through the nostrils, and the medication is pumped directly into the stomach. Usually the medicine is strong and it may cause a great bout of diarrhea. If you worm your horse on a regular basis you should not need to tube worm.

EXPLANATION OF THE EFFECT OF DRUGS

Absorbent — something that soaks up or absorbs

Alterative — a drug that changes the conditions and functions of organs

Anesthetic — a substance that causes the loss of feeling or sensation

Anodyne — a drug that soothes or diminishes pain

Antacid — a substance that counteracts the effects of acids

Anthelmintic — used to kill or expel worms

Antiperiodic — stops or detains the return of spasms in periodic diseases

Antiseptics — stops or detains the decay of tissue

Antispasmodic — a substance that prevents or lessens cramps

Aperient — a laxative used to gently open the bowels

Aromatic — a strong-smelling stimulant used to dispel gas and allay pain

Astringent — a tonic that causes contraction

Carminative — a warming stimulant that expels gas, which causes colic

Cathartic — used to freely open the bowels

Caustic — a chemical reaction that destroys tissue

Cholagogue — causes an increase in the secretion of bile

Demulcent — a soothing substance that protects irritated surfaces

Detergent — a substance that cleanses the skin

Diaphoretic — a remedy that increases the secretions of sweat

Discutient — a local application that removes the congestion of inflamed parts and the skin covering them.

Disinfectant — a chemical that destroys contagious matter

Diuretic — increases the flow of urine

Ecbolic — a drug that causes contraction of the womb

Emetic — an agent that induces vomiting

Emollient — a substance that softens and relaxes the parts whereto it is applied

Excitant — a stimulant when applied locally

Expectorant — something that aids in removing the secretions from the air passages

Febrifuge — lessens fevers and lowers temperatures

Laxative — a mild physic

Narcotic — produces sleep and allays pain

Refrigerant — an agent that diminishes heat

Sedative — an agent that exerts a soothing effect upon the system

Sialogoues — an agent that increases the secretion of saliva.

Soperific — another name for narcotic

Stimulant — a drug that temporarily excites the nevous system or the circulation

Stomachic — an improver of digestion

Tonic — an agent that improves digestion and nutrition

Vermifuge — a substance used to kill and expel worms

HOW OFTEN TO GIVE MEDICINES

Alteratives — may be given once or twice a day

Purgatives — should not be repeated under twenty-four hours, even in severe cases, and in ordinary cases, not under forty-eight hours

Tonics — should be given two or three times a day

Stimulants — if found necessary, may be repeated every three hours

Ecbolics — may be repeated after forty-five minutes

Febrifuges — medicine to reduce fever and allay fevers, should be given as often as every two or three hours in severe cases, and as often as three times a day in mild cases

2
EXERCISE

Look upon your horse as an athlete. Nature has given him a body to answer his every need, and most of a human's demands upon it. Yet, if it is out of condition, his body cannot respond fully, either to his needs or to your demands. Asking an "out of condition" horse to perform to his utmost capacity is like asking a retired track star to run a two minute mile, or an out of work dancer to perform a full length ballet. They cannot. It is impossible. Just like any other athlete, the horse needs daily exercise to keep in top shape, and, that is not meant to be a fast once-around the barn-yard, and done. Daily exercise should consist of enough work to make the horse's pulse, respiration, and perspiration output increase to the point where, at least, one of the three are noticeable. This does not mean to work an "out of condition" horse into the ground. A horse that is out of condition will sweat, breath fast, and tire very quickly, and should not be pushed too hard. His exercise time should be gradually increased each day until he no longer breathes quickly or begins to sweat readily at a given point where he did so the day before.

A good way to begin exercising a horse is to lunge him. Horses that are just being taught to lunge should be equipped with a halter that has a caveson noseband, equipped with a swivel ring on the front and side reins attached to a surcingle. The side reins will keep the horse's head set in the position that you wish it to be, and the swivel on the top of the noseband permits easy attachment of the lunge rein itself. After the horse knows what is expected of him and has become fully accustomed to lunging, you may dispense with both the caveson noseband and the side reins, and

Lunging exercises the horse when he cannot be ridden.

lunge him on his halter and lunge line alone.

To lunge a horse you should have a lunge line. This is a twenty-five foot line made either of nylon or canvas tape, the latter preferable as it is not as slippery to hold, and you should have a lunging whip that is approximately five feet long in the shaft with a lash of about four more feet. To get the horse to lunge you should stand at a right angle to him, that is, stand facing his side, just behind the point of his hip and have him on a medium length lead. If you are starting him in a left hand circle, hold the lunge rein in you left hand, the whip in your right, and move the rein forward and out from the shoulder so that he will know that that is the direction wherein he is to move. Gently touch him with the whip, just below the hocks, to start him. As he circles, give him more rein, as long as he keeps it taut. If he should be sluggish, urge him on with the whip, but do not frighten him with it. When not in use, the whip should be held so that it is touching the ground and not distracting the horse. Teach the horse voice commands by repeating vocally the gait, at which he is lunging. If you want him to walk, say walk and make him do so accordingly. The same is done with the other gaits. When changing gaits, either from slow to fast, or back again, be sure to speak your command as well as encouraging him with the rein or whip. To increase the horse's speed, lengthen the rein and speak your command along with a gentle tap with the whip. To slow him, shorten the rein and use voice commands. When lunging, make sure that the horse circles you, you should not have to walk in large circles with the horse. Also, keep out of the way of his hoofs as many horses are frisky when lunged and have a tendency to jump or kick, especially if the weather is cold or nippy. Always give equal time to lunging in both directions, as one side of the animal will become more developed than the other if you do not. Also, lunging in both directions will teach the horse to change leads and will make him equally handy with both sets of feet. Lunging is also a good way to take some of the starch out of an especially frisky or nervous horse before riding him. It is a good idea to let your horse get his bucking done before a ride, rather than during a hunt or first canter of the day. Twenty minutes on the lunge rein before a ride will steady most horses down, and you will find that the extra twenty minutes spent in lunging him before the ride is well worth not having to fight with the horse out on the trail, or in the huntfield. Lunging under saddle also gives the horse time to get rid of any air that he might have taken in while you were drawing up your girth, and relaxes

Lunging under saddle before a ride loosens and relaxes the horse.

his muscles so that you may take up on your girth before the ride. You then know that your saddle is not going to slip because he blew out his belly, and you forgot to check after mounting.

If you have difficulty in getting a horse to understand what you want him to do while lunging, have someone assist you by clipping a lead rope to the ring in the halter whereto the lunging rein is clipped, and have them lead the horse through his various gaits until he learns what you want. This is also a good way to teach the horse to stop, for it is often easier to get a horse going on a lunge line than it is to stop him once he is moving. Several times in the lunge like this and your horse should get the idea.

The other method of exercising is to ride the horse yourself. A daily ride, weather permitting, is good, not only for the horse, but for the rider as well. When leaving the stable, walk your horse for the first fifteen minutes. This allows the blood to warm up and gets his circulation going and his muscles prepared. If he is going to try any tricks, this will also be the most likely time to do it, when he is not too far from the barn and the comfort of his stall. The same applies at the end of the ride. Walk your horse for the last fifteen minutes. Or you can figure the first mile out and the last mile back. Daily exercise is a must, even if you only ride your

Daily exercise, in the form of riding, is beneficial to both the horse and you.

horse at a walk or trot around a large field near your stable, but it must be some kind of exercise that is consistent, and for at least an hour, if at all possible, to have any beneficial effects, either on the horse or you. In bad weather, when it is slippery or muddy, and you are afraid to ride, then lunging is ideal, as long as it is done no faster than a trot. You do not, of course, want the horse to slip, fall or strain muscles or ligaments in the process. If you have a large barn with a wide center aisle, the horse may be walked and trotted in hand for an hour, and though this is tedious and tiring work, it will keep both the horse and you in shape.

3
FEED

One very important aspect of horse care is the proper buying, handling, storing, and, of course, feeding of feeds to your animal. Good nutrition is especially important for getting a horse in condition and keeping him that way. One of the best ways to assure your horse of good nutrition is to select your own feeds for him, and to do that properly you should first know what to look for in feeds, what feed is right for your horse, and the type of work that he is doing. One of the most crucial things to look for when purchasing feed is freshness in grains, feeds, mixes, hays, pellets, and/or supplements. The fresher the feed, the better and higher the nutrition. However, do not confuse the word freshness for greener or uncured feeds. All feeds should be fully ripe and mature before being used in mixes, as straight feeds, or as supplements. How do you tell if feeds or grains are good and fit to feed your horse? The best idea when purchasing feed is to go directly to the feed mill and either handpick the feed and grain yourself, or approve or reject feed that has already been processed and/or bagged by the feed mill. There is only one way to do this, and that is to see, smell, and touch the feeds and grains. The feed mill may not like having to open its feed sacks for your inspection. However, unless your mill has something to hide they can hardly refuse your request. When looking for good oats you should first know what type of oats you want and need for your horse. There are several varieties, such as whole oats, crimped or crushed oats, rolled oats, and of course, your own locally grown oats. Whole oats are just what their name implies. They are whole kernels of oats that have not been split, bruised, or crushed in any way and they retain more

Fresh, whole oats.

vitamins and minerals than any other type of oat. The husk or kernel of the oat is in its natural condition, with the husk acting like a protective coating that seals in all of the nutrients produced by nature. Many horsemen advocate feeding crimped or crushed oats, as they appear to be more easily digested by the horse. However, if a horse's teeth are properly kept, that is floated once a year to provide good, strong biting surfaces and eliminate long or sharp edges that hinder his chewing, I feel that the animal should have no trouble in crushing the oat kernels and thus, gain better nutrition from the whole, natural oats.

Crimped oats are, as previously stated, oats that have had the kernels crushed or broken open. They are flattened in appearance to some degree and much of the nutrition that the oat would normally have is lost, due to contact with the air. If you feed crushed or crimped you should also feed a vitamin supplement to help replace the nutrients that have been lost.

Rolled oats are dry, flat, and look very little like an oat. Oatmeal is made from rolled oats, and although rolled oats are sometimes used in mixed feeds, they should not be used straight as a horse feed, unless specified by the veterinarian. There is very little

Crushed, or crimped oats.

nutrition to rolled oats. Most of the vitamins and minerals are lost and what remains is the fat content of the oat. When looking for oats for feed, you should be sure that the oats are full-kerneled, that is, the kernels being plump-looking and full, fairly shiny, and clean with no rusty or greyish casts to them. Oats that are good for feed will be shiny and clean, and will rustle readily when shaken in a container. The oats should not cling together, nor should they be sticky to the touch. Oats that appear to be sticky or that are reddish or grey tinged may be moldy, mildewed, or have oat blight, none being good for your horse. Also, oats should not appear to be flat-kerneled, grey, powdery, or leave a silvery grey residue on the hands when held. This is a sure sign of old oats, and old oats have very poor nutritional value. Oats that feel abrasive to the touch and that have a slight or very greenish cast to them are just that, green oats. Feeding unripe grain is one of the fastest ways to produce colic and/or founder in a horse. If the oats feel slightly raspy when rubbed in the hand, or feel as though they catch on one another, take a good long look to be sure *they are not green*.

Your sense of smell is another good indicator as to whether or not grain is fit to feed. Oats should have a nutlike scent and should never smell musty, mildew, or sour. Oats that smell like mold and mildew are more than likely just that, and oats that smell sour may have been stored while damp and may either be beginning to rot or to ferment. Green oats will not have the nutlike aroma and may, though not always, smell a bit like green grass.

A good oat to feed is one that is shiny, full-kerneled, dry, but not powdery to the touch, golden to tan in color, and rustly sounding when shaken in a small container.

Oats come in different weights, too, such as light, heavy, extra heavy, fancy, etc. Your feed mill or veterinarian will be able to help you decide which is right for your horse and the work that he will be doing.

One more thing to avoid when buying oats is kiln-dried oats. Sometimes oats will be advertised as kiln-dried and they may be less expensive than other oats. However, oats are usually kiln-dried because the oats have become wet after harvesting and often moldy as well. The kiln-drying destroys much of the nutrition as well as bleaching the oat, and many horses will refuse to eat kiln-dried grain. Also, it is not good for the horse to eat these oats, for though the mold spores will be destoyed by the kiln-drying, if they were moldy as well as wet, the fact remains that the feed was once in unfit condition for the animal.

Steamed oats should be avoided as well. Steaming is sometimes done to plump up oats that have been stored for a long time and are old. The steaming often causes the oats to begin fermenting or may cause them to mold, and if conditions are just right, the oats may begin to sprout due to the dampness of the steaming. **Never** feed a horse sprouting oats.

Oats are sometimes mixed with other things to produce mixed feed or horse feeds. Most mixed horse feeds contain the following items: linseed meal, soybean meal, crimped oats, crimped or rolled corn, cane molasses, deactivated animal sterol (source of vitamin D3, vitamin A, vitamin E, dicalcium phosphate, calcium carbonate, salt and trace minerals, as well as other carbonates, sulfates, and oxides of various minerals). Variations of mixed feeds may include: dehydrated alfalfa pellets, wheat bran, crimped barley, hominey feed, brewers grains, and/or brewers yeasts. The molasses base of the feed may be either light or heavy, depending upon the type and usage of the feed, and many mills will custom mix a feed for you, adding or subtracting anything you like or dislike. Many will also lighten or make heavier the molasses base of the feed at your order. Regardless of the type of mixed feed you use, it is essential to know just what fresh mixed feeds

Mixed horse feed.

look, smell, and feel like. As with oats, mixed feed should not only look fresh, but smell fresh as well. A good mixed feed will be sweet-smelling and will appear rich in color and texture. Depending upon the amount of molasses in the base, the mix will hold together to some degree after being squeezed in the hand. The lighter the molasses base, the less the mix will cling together, and of course the heavier the base the more packing will occur. At no time should a mixed feed smell sour, silagelike, be black or grey in color, nor should it be tacky and/or gummy in texture. A good mix will leave small bits of itself clinging on the palm of the hand after being squeezed, but the bits should be easily dusted from the hand by brushing the palms together. Feed that is black in color may be rotting. Feed that is grey in color may be old, moldy or mildewed. Feed that smells sour or silage like is starting to ferment. Feed top quality, fresh mixed feed to your horses.

Horses that are allergic to grains and dust that is sometimes connected with oats and hay, may be fed specially prepared horse chows. These are processed to produce as little dust as possible, and still be palatable and nutritious to your horse. Pelleted feeds may also replace the horse's hay when need be, such as in the special treatment required in cases of heaves. The pelleted hays are usually vitamin charged to give added nutrition, as are most of the mixed feeds and chows.

Alfalfa pellets.

Vitamin supplements may be required at times. Perhaps you want to show your horse and he needs to have extra stamina, or a better coat than nature alone could give him. At times like these, a vitamin supplement is a good thing to have around. Also, a vitamin supplement cannot be surpassed for getting an ailing horse back on his feet, or for building strong bones and energy in a foal that is still developing in the mare. Special supplements are available for lactating mares, and for weanlings or growing foals, as well as for all-around conditioning of any horse. Supplements come in a variety of forms, just as feeds do. Some are powdered, oils, pellets, or granules, and most of the supplements will aid in producing a glossier coat and more hoof growth. However, before you feed any supplement to your horse, discuss his overall condition with your vet to be sure that he does, in fact, need a supplement. Many horses with poor coats could do with less supplements and better grooming, and a more frequently filled water bucket. Consult your vet to see what is right for your horse. One thing to watch for, however, if you do feed a supplement, is that your horse is not gaining weight faster than he should, or gaining more weight that he should. Some supplements, as well as mixed feeds, are high in fat content, and a horse that is normally healthy can gain weight very quickly on some of these products. Also, a horse that has been foundered should never be fed mixed feed because of the heating properties found in the mixes. Most mixes have a tendency to heat the horse's blood somewhat, due to the high energy content, and this is not good for a horse that has been foundered. Some horses, that are very sensitive, may also break out in small pimples if their feed is too rich. If this happens and you are feeding a mixed feed, either change the mix for one with a lower richness, or change to oats instead. Remember, when changing from one feed to another, do it gradually. Never make a sudden change from one feed to another as your horse's system needs time to adapt to new levels of fat, vitamins, minerals, and other feed elements.

Other supplements to feeds that may be mixed with oats when you do not wish to buy mixed feed are barley, and split, dried beans. Barley should be rolled, as it is very hard, but both barley and dried beans provide added nutrition and oils to the feed. Also, neither are very heating to the horse's blood.

Rolled barley, ready to be mixed with oats.

Bran, too, is sometimes used as a supplement or in bran mashes. Bran is slightly laxative and may be used in treating the early stages of founder. It is cooling, soothing, and may be given in hot bran mashes after hard work, such as hunting, to ease a tired horse. To make a bran mash, mix two or three quarts of bran with enough boiling water to make it about the consistency of thick oatmeal. Mix it in a pail, add a teaspoon of salt and a few cut up carrots, and cover with a feed sack or other partially porous cloth. Allow the mixture to steam until it is cool enough to eat.

When buying bran, good bran should be loose when handled and should leave a slightly floury residue on the hands when picked up. It should never lump or cling together, for this shows that the bran is damp.

A salt block is another good thing to give your horse. Many horses tend to chew on things in an attempt to correct a salt deficiency in their systems. A large salt block placed in the pasture or a small block in the stall will replace the salt lost by the horse when he perspires. Salt is necessary in every healthy horse's diet.

Now, what about hay? The most standard type of hay for horses is timothy grass. This hay agrees with more horses than any other

Pasture-size salt block.

type of grass used for hay, and it has a good level of nutrition. A mix of alfalfa and timothy may also be fed, but the amount of alfalfa in the mix should be carefully watched, because alfalfa is a laxative, and too much of it can scour your horse's bowels. If you have a horse that has trouble with constipation, however, and you are sure that the problem is not caused by too little drinking water or worms, then an alfalfa/timothy mix may be the answer. Alfalfa is also very high in protein and vitamins.

Now, what should hay look like? Timothy has narrow leaves and long, thin heads with no flowers like clover or alfalfa hay. The hay will be a dull green, but not grey or yellowish in color. It should smell like dried grass, but should never smell wet, moldy, or green. To inspect a bale of hay you should first feel it. The hay should be springy to the touch and not be too brittle. The stalks should have a certain amount of toughness and should not come apart readily, or easily be broken or pulled from the bale. Hay that crumbles or snaps easily from the bale is old and will usually have little odor, and the color often becomes brown or greyish. Hay that smells wet or green may not have been properly dried before baling and oftentimes the center of the bale will be moldy. When opened, a moldy bale of hay will be dark in the center, sometimes

Clean, well-baled timothy hay.

having stringy, whitish, threadlike matter running through it, and in bales that have been moldy for a long time, the center of the bale may even be slimy to the touch. Moldy hay smells very strongly of the mold, smelling wet and sometimes slightly rotten, and it should never be fed to a horse, or any other animal for that matter. If a bale has been moldy and the mold has dried, rather than causing the bale to rot, the inner parts or sections of hay will be coated with a grey residue that will often fly about when the hay is pulled apart. Even dried mold can be scented, and if you open a bale and it contains dried mold, again it should not be fed to your animals.

How will you know if a bale is moldy before you open it? Well, sometimes it is a bit difficult to tell, but one way is to look at the rest of the bale. If the bale appears to be sound, well cured, and has a good color, it should be a good bale. However, one test you can make is to force your hands as far down into the middle of the bale as you can, then bend close and smell the hay where your hands have entered the bale. Many times mold and mildew can be scented in this manner. Also, ask your feed mill manager where he stores the hay and whether his storage area is weathertight. Hays that are stored outside or in open lofts, often get wet or damp, and these will be the first to mold. Also, as with feed of any type, hay should not be stored for more that one year, as feeds and grains loose nutrition with time and good nutrition is all-important for a healthy horse.

Now, what about feed and grain storage? The best way to store grains and feeds is in a feed box. One of the best types of feed boxes is the wooden, slant-top variety. The slant-top fits flush at both the sides and front of the box, making it extremely difficult for a horse to open, however, take no chances, for many horses are very adept with lips, teeth, and tongue. Keep all feeds and hays stored properly in the feed room or feed barn. By the way, it is best to keep all feeds and grains stored either in a separate room on the floor level of the barn or, better yet, in a seperate building altogether. This cuts down on the fire hazards.

Other good storage containers are galvanized garbage cans, metal overseas chests, plastic garbage cans, and fiber drums. The best of these are the galvanized garbage cans and metal overseas chests. They are usually tightly constructed and keep out dampness very well. Plastic garbage pails do well, but are easily chewed through by rodents. Fiber drums are good if used for short term storage only, that is, if you use a lot of feed in a short amount of time. The fiber drums tend to hold moisture and will quickly

Solid, slant-top feed bin for grain storage.

Small, well-capped haystack, waiting to be used.

cause feed to become damp if the feed is not used rapidly.

Hay should be stored in baled stacks in a dry place with the bales being piled in alternate positions, the two center bales being left out in the second row, the bales next to the ends of the row left out in the third row, and so on. This allows for ventilation of the stacked bales and cuts down on the risk of spontaneous combustion. Hay may be stored loose outside if stacked in a haystack, but only if the stack is properly capped and the hay used in the capping discarded when the stack is broken open for use. Proper building of a haystack takes a lot of practise, and is fast becoming a dying art in this country.

You may have noticed that so far I have not mentioned the use of corn as a feed. Corn should not be used straight as a feed, except when your horse is doing particularly heavy or hard work, such as daily fox hunting, and even then, the amount fed should be carefully controlled. Corn is very fattening and most horses are better off without it. Another exception to this is the sick or highly undernourished horse that needs building up, and again, the amount of corn fed should be closely supervised. If you do have reason to feed corn, then the corn that is fed should be of the highest quality. Corn that is to be used for feed may be purchased either in loose, bulk form, or still on the cob. The corn on the cob is a good idea as it gives the horse's teeth good exercise when he bites it off. Cob corn should be deep yellow, shiny with plump kernels and should be dry and smooth to the touch. Kernels should not feel soft or damp. There should be no black or dark grey matter between the rows, or clinging to the kernels of corn. Black or grey matter may be a sign of corn smut or corn affected with mold, and this should not be fed to the horse. Also, corn that feels soft and appears damp or green should be avoided as feed.

Loose corn may be either in whole kernels or rolled. The rolled form will be flattened out, the kernels broken open, and much of the shininess and golden color will be gone, due to the crushing process. Corn like this is most often used to add to a mix, or used when a horse has some sort of mouth difficulty or chewing problem, most commonly due to age.

Corn is best stored in a wooden feed bin, perhaps a double feed bin with one side for oats and one side for corn. It keeps the feed more or less together and cuts down on the feeding chores. The next best storage idea for corn is to keep it in a galvanized garbage can.

As you can see feed is a very important part of horse care. As important as the feed itself, is knowing how and when to feed. The best idea for feeding is three times a day as the horse has a very small stomach for its size, and does best when given small, frequent meals. However, twice a day feeding schedules are more commonly followed than the three times a day schedules. Let us suppose, however, that you intend to feed three times a day. The feed should be split into the following ration. One-fourth of the days allowance should be given at breakfast, one-fourth at lunch, and the other half at suppertime. Since the horse will have to be without food for the greatest time during the night, it is best to see that he goes to bed with a "full belly." Feeding the largest meal at night, in reality gives the horse something to do during a time when there is no stable activity. Hay given at night often lasts well into the late hours and keeps the horse satisfied.

Now, however, let us suppose that your schedule does not permit a three time a day feeding schedule, as is usually the case, and you have to do as most of us do, feed twice a day instead. In this instance you should divide the grain or feed ration in half, feeding half at breakfast and half at supper. The hay ration should be divided into one-fourth for morning and three-quarters for evening. This does nearly the same thing as three times a day feeding, by feeding the greater amount of bulk, the hay, at night and thus, keeping the horse satisfied. Should you happen to be lucky enough to be able to get home during your lunch hour, you might want to split the grain ration into one-half morning, one-half at night, and the hay ration into one-quarter in the morning, one-quarter at noon, and one-half at night. This, too, leaves a greater part of the feed for evening. Supplements should be added to the feed as directed. However, I find that feeding a supplement in the morning cuts down on the chances of the horse leaving it. Most horses are a bit hungrier in the mornings and are not as inclined to be choosy about what is added to their feeds.

Naturally, your horse should have access to water, whether from an automatic fountain in his stall, or from a water bucket. He should be able to drink whenever he wishes. This keeps him from becoming dehydrated or excessively thirsty, and thus, bolting the water when he gets it. A horse that does not have water at all times will often develop impacted bowels, or may drink himself sick when given access to water. Also, horses that have water all the time will regulate their water intake properly, but a horse without water will not. A horse that does not have water all the time should be watered before he is fed, and then not again until an hour after feeding. Watering before feeding allows the water to pass from the stomach, and thus, will not interfere with digestion. Watering too soon after feeding causes the feed and grain to be washed out of the stomach before it is fully digested, and may cause packing down and fermentation of food in the bowels. This will ultimately cause colic. This is why it is best, if at all possible, to provide free access to water at all times, as the horse will then drink only at the proper times and should have no trouble with either his stomach or bowels.

4
BEDDING

Another aspect of good horse care is the bedding that you select and use in your horse's stall. Naturally, you want him to stay as clean and dry as possible. The type of bedding you select will be all-important in keeping the horse both comfortable and clean. First, you should decide what type of bedding you want to use, and there are a variety of substances available for this purpose. One

Fresh clean shavings awaiting use as stall bedding.

thing that ranks very high on the list of good bedding is wood shavings. These are simply thin curls of wood that have been planed from a larger piece of wood, and they are usually found in great abundance at planing mills, cabinet makers, and some lumber yards that do their own mill work. In many instances, these establishments will let you take as much of their shavings as you want, as most mills are glad to have a place to dispose of their shavings. Some mills will charge a small fee if they have to put the shavings in a container for you, but most charge nothing as long as you bag, or otherwise package the shavings yourself.

Now, what should you look for in the way of shavings? First of all, they should be dry to the touch or very nearly so, and should not smell sour, be dark in color, or wet and sticky to the touch. Darkness, wetness, and sour odor are all signs that the shavings are beginning to rot or otherwise go bad. In order to be good as bedding and to keep the stall as clean and dry as possible, the shavings must be dry themselves. If the shavings are only slightly damp and no others are available, then you should spread them out somewhere to dry when you get them home. It does not take shavings long to dry when spread thinly on a dry surface. Once dried, they may then be placed in the area that you are going to use as storage for them. A clean, airy, unused stall is an ideal place to store shavings. Large fiber drums are also good containers for storing shavings, but like feed, only for a short period of time, say for a few days. Here again, if the weather is damp, the fiber tends to hold the dampness and the shavings may become wet and/or limp. Good shavings should be pale in color, crisp, and should rustle. These are the best shavings and will absorb much of the stall moisture. Shavings also do not have a tendency to pack down or cake as do some other types of beddings. The shavings allow much of the moisture to be absorbed from them and into the ground floor of the stall below them. Too, droppings are easily seen in the shavings and can be removed each time they are seen. This enables you to keep the stall clean, without having to clean the whole stall, and a cleaner kept stall means a cleaner horse.

Sometimes the shavings are mixed with sawdust, and while this is not an ideal situation, it is acceptable for bedding. Sawdust, however, tends to pack and cake and will get in the horse's coat, often making him appear dusty and dirty, even right after grooming. Too, it has a tendency to be fly away when the humidity in the air is low, and can be inhaled easily by the animal, thus, setting up the possibility of respiratory trouble. Sawdust should never be used alone, for all of the above reasons, and because it makes a very heavy load when cleaning the stall, as well as becoming nearly rock hard by the end of the week, due to the horse walking over the damp bedding and packing it down.

Another good substance to use for bedding is peat moss. While peat does make an excellent bedding, in that it is highly absorbant, and does not fly away and will not pack down, there is one drawback to its use. It is quite expensive, as all peat moss used in America is imported. Too, while being an excellent bedding it is not one of the most attractive substances to use because of its rather dark color, and the bed is not all that attractive when made up. Too, it is sometimes harder to see the droppings at a glance, as one can with shavings. However, if you do not mind spending more time to look harder for the droppings, then peat moss makes an ideal bedding.

Straw, of course, is a popular bedding and is one of the most widely used. Wheat straw is the most commonly used because it is the least palatable of straws and the most readily available. Straw should be golden to pale yellow in color, and should flake out readily from the bale when the bale is broken open for use. The pats or sections of straw should never cling tenaciously together in lumps or clumps, nor should they be dark or damp toward the

Clean, fresh straw which is also a popular bedding.

A freshly opened bale of moldfree straw.

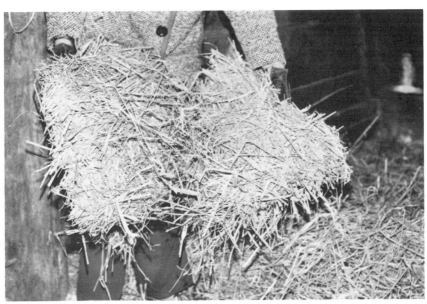

Straw will be crisp and readily separated when fit for use as horse bedding.

middle of the bale. As with the hay, the straw should smell fresh, never musty or moldy, and like hay, should never be used for bedding if mold and mildew are present.

Many horses have a tendency to eat their bedding, often from sheer boredom, and should a horse do so with moldy bedding, the consequences could be rather severe.

Good straw will be shiny when spread on the stall floor, and will oftentimes be slippery under foot. Again, droppings should be removed from the bed as soon as they are seen, and before they have a chance to become buried under other straw, or collect in large mats. The one bad thing about using straw for bedding is that it has a tendency to collect on the droppings, matting into them, and they are sometimes difficult to see. Straw does, however afford good absorption and drainage, and if kept clean, the horse will remain clean as well. Also, there is little dust or dirt connected with straw and the horse will not have the tendency to become dusty-looking.

A more recent addition to the bedding market is a product called *Staz-dry*. This is specially prepared bedding that is produced from denatured sugarcane waste. It comes in bales, either paper protected or plain. and it can be used exactly like shavings

Manure should never be allowed to accumulate like this between stall cleanings.

A bale of Staz-dry, another type of stall bedding.

Notice the fibrous, pulpy stems that readily absorb stall wetness.

or straw. The bales are tightly compressed, of a light to medium tan in color, and shreddy in appearance. *Staz-dry* absorbs well, does not mold, does not hold stable odors as does straw, and is lightweight and easy to handle when cleaning out the stall. Most feed mills and some tack shops handle this horse care product.

Now, how should one clean out or muck out a stall and when? Proper stable routine for keeping a stall clean is as follows: First, all dropping done during the night should be removed before the horse's breakfast is fed. Manure should never be allowed to collect for more than one day's time. After the horse has eaten he will more than likely again produce droppings that should also be removed. If you have time during the day, check on him again, and again remove whatever is present. At suppertime the routine should continue and you should give the stall one last check before retiring for the night, both to remove droppings and to freshen the water in the stall, if it is not automatic. Once a week, the entire stall should be mucked out, right down to the floor, and there is a certain knack to this if it is to be done economically and efficiently. To begin with, you should remove the horse from the stall and either turn him out to run, or place him in another stall that is empty at that time. It is much easier to clean out the stall if

One fault of straw is that it tends to mat in the manure.

the horse is not in it, though if necessity dictates that you must keep the horse in the stall while you clean it, the task is possible, though unhandy.

Let us assume that the horse has been removed from the stall and you are now ready to begin the cleaning-out operation. The first order of business is to see just how much clean dry bedding is in the stall, regardless of whether it is straw, peat moss, or shavings. All of the dry bedding should be gathered up and placed, either in a spare wheelbarrow, or in the aisle beside you. When you are sure that you removed all of the clean, dry, reusable bedding, you can begin to muck out the rest of the stall. Be sure to clean well into the stall corners and right down to the floor itself. When you have thoroughly cleaned out the stall you should spread sweet lime on the floor to sweeten it, and this should be spread well enough so that it is easily seen, yet not so thick that it might be shoveled or raked away. While you are at it, now is a good time to thoroughly clean out the manger if you have one, and the feed tub or box. If you are using the plastic type of feed tub, it should be removed from the holder and thoroughly scrubbed out with soap and water, rinsed, and dried, then rehung. This should be done once a week, preferably on the day you clean out the stall. Water buckets, too, should be thoroughly scrubbed with hot water, but with no soap, and reinstalled on cleaning day.

Now you are ready to put down a fresh bed for your horse. You should begin by placing the bedding that you saved in the center of the stall, spread out what you have, and then begin to add fresh bedding from there. Bedding should be thick enough so that you do not feel the floor of the stall when you walk around on it and should always be banked a bit higher in the corners. When removing the droppings on a daily basis, you should always see that you remove as little bedding along with the droppings as possible. The less bedding thrown away with the stall waste, the less expensive it will be for you in the long run. As you daily remove the manure you can freshen your horse's bed by bringing some of the bedding that is piled up around the edges of the stall into the center, thus keeping the horse's bed clean and dry and comfortable for him.

Now that you have finished cleaning the stall and bedding it down, it is ready once again to house your horse.

TOOLS NEEDED FOR STALL CLEANING

Wheelbarrow or muck basket	Rake
Flat shovel for floor	Pointed shovel for corners

Scrub brush for buckets
Sweet lime

Towel for drying
Fresh bedding

Newly laid straw should be placed well up in the stall corners.

5
GROOMING

Grooming is an essential daily care for the horse. Without daily grooming, a horse may soon lose his bloom, his looks, and even his health. Daily grooming loosens and removes dead hair, dirt that has accumulated in his coat, it stimulates the skin and circulation, and even increases muscle tone to some degree. Too, daily grooming stimulates the production of oil that gives the coat luster and shine. When ungroomed for a long period of time, the horse's skin becomes dry, flaky, and may cause the animal to begin rubbing against objects in an attempt to scratch the irritating itch produced by the dry skin and dandruff that he will most likely have. This scratching may open the way for skin infections and parasites, should the horse rub himself open in the process. Daily grooming of the horse is like the daily combing and brushing of your hair and teeth . You feel more comfortable after you have combed and brushed your hair and brushed your teeth in the morning, and your horse feels better after a good grooming.

A complete and proper grooming kit contains the following items:

A rubber or mud curry	Sweat Scraper
Dandy brush	Sponges (large & small)
Body or finishing brush	Hoof pick
Shedding blade	Stable rubber
Face brush	Bottle of baby oil
Pastern brush (optional)	Hand clippers

Grooming your horse should not be a quick, haphazard thing. You should not groom your horse one way one time and another way another time. Like anything else that is done around horses, grooming should be done in a set pattern. Most horses do best on a well-planned, well layed out schedule and system, where things vary little from day to day. At least as far as stable procedure goes. Let us assume that you have never groomed a horse before and you want to learn how to do so from start to finish, with the greatest efficiency and best results. The first thing to do is to tie your horse, either in a crosstie area or in a place where he is not going to be startled or unduly annoyed by anything that comes into his range of vision. Select a quiet spot and make sure that the object where you tie him to is substantial. This is not to suggest that the horse is going to try to escape from your grooming attempts, but it is to keep him in one place and make it easier for you to work on him. After all, you cannot do a good job on him if you are chasing him around the stable yard while trying to brush him. Though this may sound funny, it is a fact that the horse has a very short attention span, and he will become bored very quickly. If not tied securely, he will most likely just turn and wander off until something else catches his attention.

Next, after he is tied, let him smell the object that you are going to be working with.

Always show your horse the equipment that is going to be used on him so that he is not frightened by it.

The shedding blade.

The most common position when in use; doubled over in a loop.

Now, to begin grooming you will first need the shedding blade. This is a flat piece of metal that has one flat edge and one edge made up of a row of small combing teeth. The blade usually has a leather handle at either end and it may be used open, in both hands, or bent into a loop shape and held in one hand. The shedding blade is used to remove shedding hair and is used in the direction that the hair grows. Light to semi-medium pressure is advised, as the teeth, though small, are fairly sharp, and you do not want to nick the horse's skin with them. The shedding blade should only be used on parts of the body where bones are not close to the surface. Beginning at the poll, the shedding blade may be used on the neck, muscled parts of the shoulder and heavily fleshed parts of the back. Care should be taken not to use to blade over the backbone if it protrudes, as it might in an older horse. Care is also advised in the amount of pressure used when using the blade over the area of the kidneys. Heavier pressure may be used over the flanks and haunches, as the skin is thickest there. The shedding blade should not be used on or below knees or hocks, and never on the face or inside the thighs. Care must also be taken when using the blade on the belly and throat.

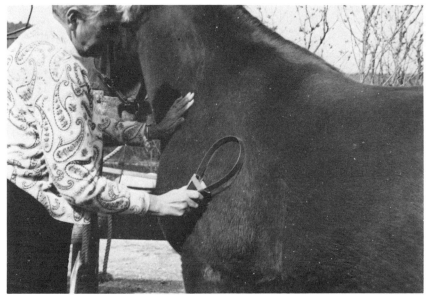

Only use the shedding blade on highly fleshed or muscled parts of the horse's body.

Exercise care on areas of thinner skin.

More pressure may be applied where the skin is thickest.

The Rubber or Mud curry.

The mud or rubber curry is exactly what the name implies. It is a rubber curry that is used in the removal of mud or caked manure from the horse's body. A circular tool, the rubber curry is usually made of rather stiff, black rubber with a hand strap. The curry has rows of circular, fairly large, blunt rubber teeth. Used in a circular motion on the horse's body, the rubber teeth loosen dead hair, caked mud, and manure. Care must be taken in its use on bony parts of the body. The face, hocks, knees, and insides of thighs should never be rubbed with the rubber curry. If mud is present in caked form on knees or hocks, it should be softened with warm water then either removed by hand, or washed away with a sponge. The legs should then be dried by pressing with a towel.

Using the rubber curry, begin at the poll and, using a circular motion, proceed to groom toward the rear of the horse, using medium pressure. Take care when using the curry on the animal's throat, loins, and belly.

The next brush to use is the dandy brush. The dandy looks much like a large scrub brush with coarse bristles set into a wooden backing. The bristles are about three inches long and are usually fibrous. Natural boar bristle brushes or rice root bristles are best for your horse, rather than nylon ones, as natural bristles

Begin on the horse's neck.

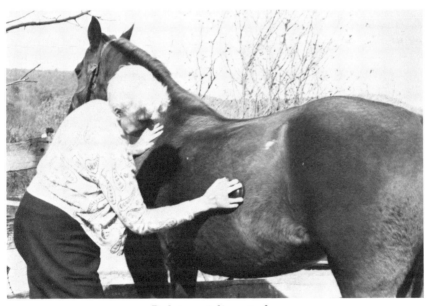

Rub in swirling strokes.

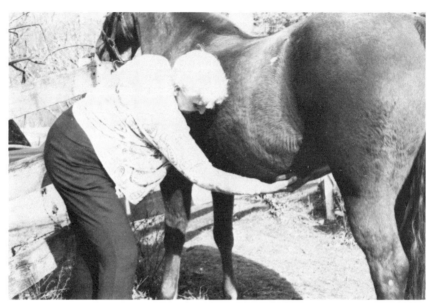

Again, take care of the amount of pressure used on sensitive areas.

More pressure may be needed on flanks and haunches.

Never use the curry below the hocks.

The Dandy brush.

do not have the tendency to split the horse's hair, like the artificial bristles.

Beginning at the horse's poll, brush in short to medium length strokes, the way the hair grows, towards the rear of the animal. Use medium to heavy pressure, depending upon what part of the horse you are working on. Use less pressure where the horse is sensitive, such as the lower belly, inside the thighs, over the loins, etc. Use more pressure where the hide is thicker such as neck, flanks, sides etc. Brushing toward the rear of the horse, continue until the loose hair and dirt have been removed and brushed away. Now and then, it is advisable to clean the bristles of the brush by dragging them across the teeth of a flat, metal curry. The metal curry is as flat plate of metal that has rows of metal teeth running across it. It has a handle whereby it is held, and should be used only for cleaning brushes. You should never use the metal curry on the horse's body. It is strictly for cleaning brushes.

Always begin grooming at the front of the animal and work backwards.

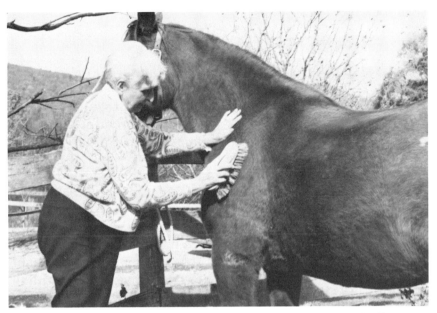

Placing the free hand against the horse while grooming him will allow you to feel any sudden movements coming before he makes them.

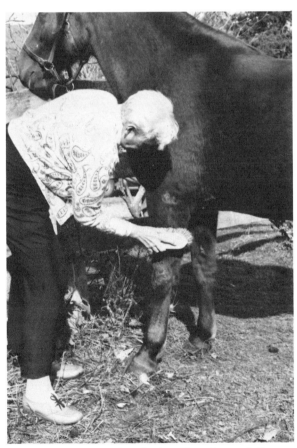

Legs should be brushed well and carefully.

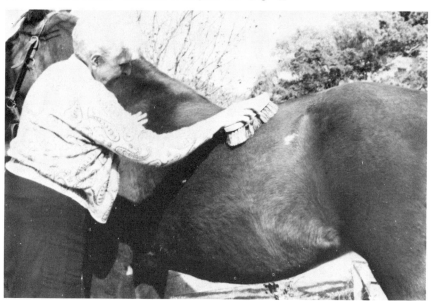

Particular attention should be paid to getting the saddle area clean.

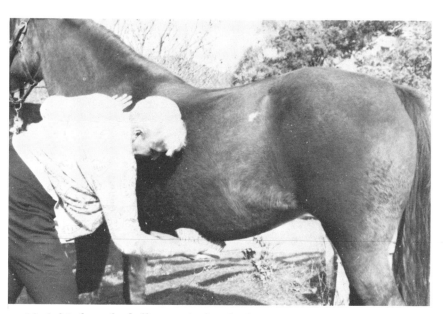

Mud dried on the belly may be brushed away easily with the dandy.

Firm pressure may be used on the horse's rear, as long as he is not touchy around the hindquarters.

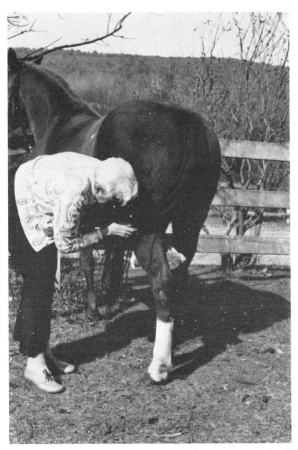

Do not neglect to brush between the hind legs or inside the hocks.

Care should always be exercised when bending near the horse's hoofs.

The metal curry, used to clean the brushes. Shown here being used to clean a Dandy brush.

The metal curry, with its sharp rows of teeth, must never be used on the horse's body.

When you have finished with the dandy brush you should next take up the body or finishing brush. This is a large, flat, oval shaped brush with short bristles set into a leather back. Beginning as you do with most of the grooming, at the poll, brush the way the hair grows, toward the rear of the animal in medium to long strokes. The body brush slicks the hair down and produces a gloss on the coat. Pressure is best at medium to heavy. As with the dandy brush, the finishing brush may be used on all parts of the horse's body. By now you should know where your horse is sensitive and where heavier pressures do not bother him. If he lowers his ears at any time during the brushing, or makes signs of moving away from you, or tries to avoid the brush, it is an indication that you are brushing too hard.

The next brushes to use are listed in the grooming kit, but may be considered optional, though personally I have found them to be invaluable for total grooming. The first is the pastern brush. This is a small brush, about the size of a nail brush for humans, but shaped more like a miniature dandy brush. This brush will most likely be found in the supermarket or hardware store, rather than in tack shops, but it is very useful. If for any reason, you have

The Body or finishing brush.

The body brush places all of the hairs of the coat in the direction of growth.

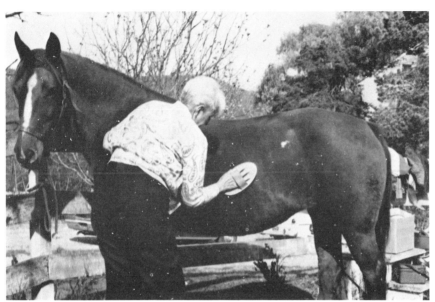

The fine bristles slick the hair down and produce a shine on the coat.

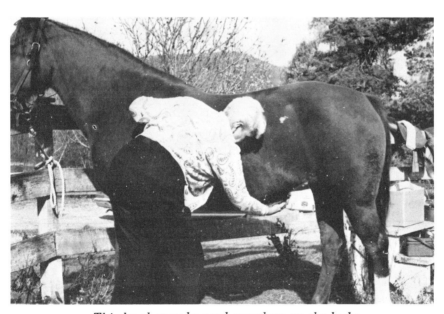

This brush may be used anywhere on the body.

As long as the horse does not resist you, you are not pressing too hard.

The finishing brush removes fine dust and dirt from legs.

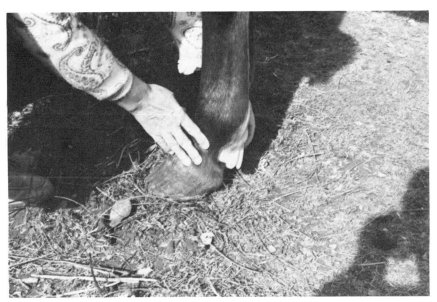

The small pastern brush is the ideal size for removing dirt from the pastern area.

allowed the hair to remain on your horse's pasterns, the pastern brush is very handy for removing mud and dirt that collects there. Being a very small brush, it easily fits into the hollow of the pastern, and you can do a very thorough job of cleaning them. Pressure should be light to medium, as the pastern skin is inclined to be sensitive in most horses. If the hair is trimmed away from the pasterns, the brush is great for removing mud and burrs that may have attached themselves or dried in the pastern area. It is also very useful for removing the flaky skin that is often found on the coronet.

The other brush that is nearly indispensable is the face brush. This brush looks like a dandy brush, also, but is about one-third smaller in size, and the bristles are very soft. This may or may not be found in tack shops, depending upon their demand for them, but you may be able to purchase them in hardware or houseware stores. To use the face brush, you start at the whorl of hair that marks the center of the horse's forehead and begin by brushing upward with the hair. Be sure when you brush the face, to shield the eyes with one hand while brushing with the other. This keeps dirt, dust and loose bits of straw, etc. from dropping into the eyes as it is brushed away from the face. The ears should be brushed

The Face brush.

Shield the horse's eyes when brushing the face.

next. Many horses do not like having their ears handled, most of them because the ears have been handled roughly sometime before. However, if you are patient and gentle with the animal, and if you take your time, eventually the horse will stop protesting when you handle his ears. When you brush the ears, always follow the direction of the hair growth, that is, brush from base to tip. The hair inside the ears may also be brushed, but do so with extreme care, as the horse's ears are very sensitive. One good pull on an ear may undo all you have done in getting him to allow you to handle his ears. When you have finished with the ears, go back to the forehead whorl of hair and begin to brush downward, this time shielding the animal's nostrils with one hand. Just as you do not want the dirt and dust to drop into his eyes, you also do not want him to breathe the dust and dirt that you are removing from his coat. Do the entire face with the face brush.

The next step is the hoof pick. This is a hook-shaped metal tool that is used to clean the horse's hoofs. The front edge of the hook is blunted and tapered so that it fits into the angles of the hoof without cutting or damaging it. To properly clean a horse's hoof, stand alongside the horse, facing the rear, and sliding your hand down his leg to the fetlock, make him lift his hoof for you. Placing

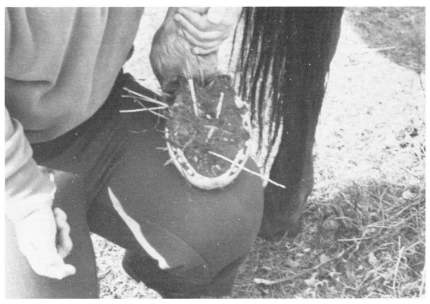

A good way to support a hind foot for cleaning.

Always begin cleaning the hoof at the heel.

your hand under the front of the lifted hoof and supporting it, you should now be looking down onto the sole of the hoof. Taking the hoof pick in the other hand, begin cleaning the hoof by scraping out any mud, manure, or foreign objects that are held by the hoof. Begin at the heel of the hoof and work forward, scraping with enough pressure to remove the accumulated matter, but not hard enough that you scratch up the sole itself. If the horse attempts to remove his hoof from your grasp while you are cleaning it, perhaps you are using too much pressure. Foundered horses will be more pressure sensitive than others. Be sure to clean the cleft of the frog and the area around it well, for it is here that thrush starts. *Never* clean the hoof from toe to heel. This will only drive the dirt and manure deeper into the frog area, and you may damage the sensitive skin of the heels in this manner. Clean well the area around the edge of the shoe. Small bits of manure tend to cling there, and should not be allowed to remain. Also, check for small stones or other foreign matter that may have become lodged under the edge of the shoe. If your horseshoes fit properly this should not happen. However, it is a good idea to check just the same, for if allowed to remain, these tiny stones may imbed themselves in the foot, due to the horse walking on them, and may cause lameness.

Scrape forward, from heel to toe.

NEVER use the pick in this manner; from toe towards the heel.

Clean well around the area where the shoe meets the hoof.

If your horse is unshod, check the area of the wall of the foot. See that the wall and the sole are firmly bound to each other and that nothing has penetrated or separated them. Also, whether shod or unshod, each time you clean the hoofs you should make a check of the hoofs to see that pieces of the wall have not been broken and are not shelling away, either from the wall or from around the front of the shoe. Having a farrier's rasp is handy in cases like this, as the broken spots or pieces of hoof wall that may be sticking up, may be filed smooth until the blacksmith can get there to trim or reset the feet and shoes. By filing them away, you reduce the chance of the piece of hoof catching on something and tearing further. After all of the hoofs have been picked out, you are ready to begin combing the mane and tail.

This area of grooming seems to be one of great disagreement among horsemen, as some advocate using a brush and never a metal comb on mane and tail, while others advocate just the opposite, using a metal comb and never a brush. In either case, a good way to begin grooming both mane and tail is to take a bit of baby oil in your hand and apply it to the root of the mane, or tail, whichever you happen to be grooming. Let us begin with the

A well cleaned out hoof.

A bit of baby oil applied to the mane helps alleviate dryness.

Groom small sections of the mane at one time.

mane. Starting at the poll, if you have not trimmed a place out for the bridle, or at the front of the mane if you have, add a little baby oil to the hair, taking just a small section of mane, then taking either brush or comb, which ever you happen to prefer, begin to brush or comb the separated section of hair. If your horse has a very thick mane, I think you will do better with a metal comb for this will separate the hair better and will comb completely, rather than just slicking the top hair of the mane. Taking small sections of hair at a time, work your way down the length of the mane. If the mane is very thick, you might find it helpful to flip the mane over so that it lies on the sides of the neck opposite the side it usually lies on. Now, taking sections of hair from what will be the underside of the mane when lying naturally, begin combing it out on the side where it will lie when finished. It is important, especially with thick manes, to comb both the top and undersides of the mane. If you find that the hair is tangled or very dry and full of static, or that it is fly away, continue to add small amounts of baby oil as you go. This not only helps to condition the hair, but it makes combing easier and cuts down on hair breakage. Use the baby oil sparingly, that is, do not soak the hair with it, for too much will cause bedding to cling to the hair. Used properly, however, it will be absorbed by the roots of the hair and that also tends to cut down on dandruff in the mane. Continue to comb or brush the mane until you have it lying completely straight, smooth, and flat against the neck. Brushing seems to work better than combing on horses with thin, wispy manes and tails. Now you should brush or comb out the forelock, again using the baby oil if necessary.

Next is the tail. A bit of baby oil rubbed into the roots of the hair at the top of the tail at each grooming, will often cure the horse of rubbing his tail into frizzies, if dry skin is making him do so. However, it will do nothing if his problem is worms. Many horses develop dry skin at the base of the tail and will rub against their mangers, etc. to relieve the itching produced by them. It is sometimes difficult to tell if the itching is caused by dry skin or by worms. However, if dry skin is the cause, then baby oil will relieve it.

Beginning at the top of the tail, begin to comb or brush downward toward the end of the tail. Always comb or brush the hair in the direction that it grows. One of the best ways to groom a thick tail is to drape it over your shoulder and section it out like you did with the mane. Working with small sections of hair at a time

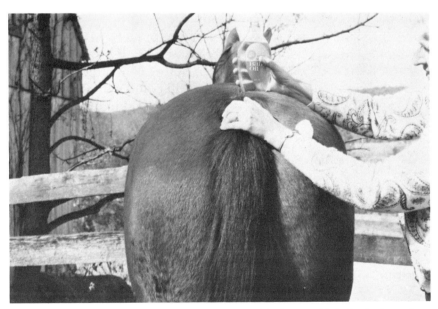

Baby oil applied to the dock or root of the tail helps to slick the hair and stop dryness of the skin.

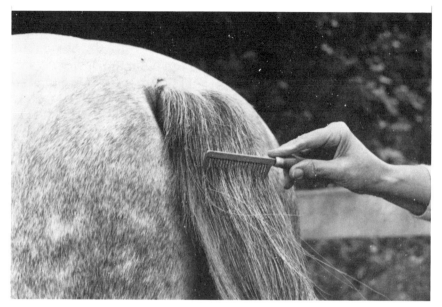

Metal combs are good in thick hair.

Long tails are best combed out in sections.

makes it easier to see that you are getting all of the hair properly combed out, and that you are not leaving any burrs, straw, shaving, etc. in the tail. Should you find burrs in the tail, you should remove them by hand, pulling the hair free of the burr, and not by pulling the burr away from the tail. By pulling the hair away from the burr, you decrease the chance of the hair splitting or breaking. All foreign matter should be removed from the tail in the above manner and not combed or brushed away.

When you have several sections of hair completely free of mats, burrs, etc., and they are completely combed out, take them and comb them together in the position wherein they will hang when you are finished. Then proceed to the rest of the tail, continuing in the same manner as before, until the entire tail has been groomed and hangs in its natural position. All tangles and mats in manes and tails should be removed by hand. If they are too thickly matted, the mane and forelock should be roached or cut off.

The next grooming item is the sponge. Taking the small sponge, wring it out in warm water and clean the area around the eyes and nostrils, washing out any dirt or dust that has accumulated there. Be gentle, for the face is sensitive. Next, take the larger sponge and wring it out in warm water, and wash the dock of the horse's

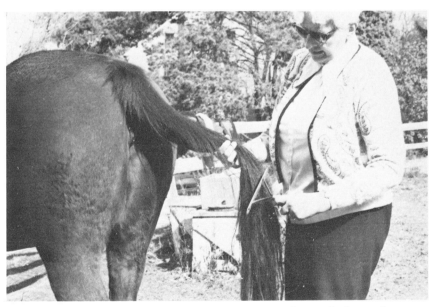

After all tangles are removed, the hair may be combed together.

Snarls in manes and tails should be loosened and removed by hand.

A forelock completely matted with burrs.

Roaching is the only solution to this particular problem.

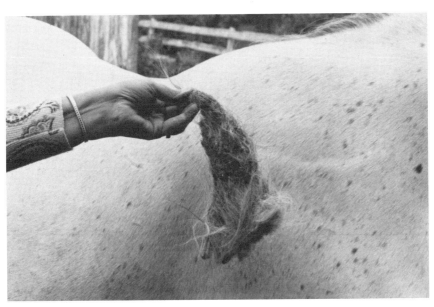

Lack of daily grooming necessitated the removal of this forelock.

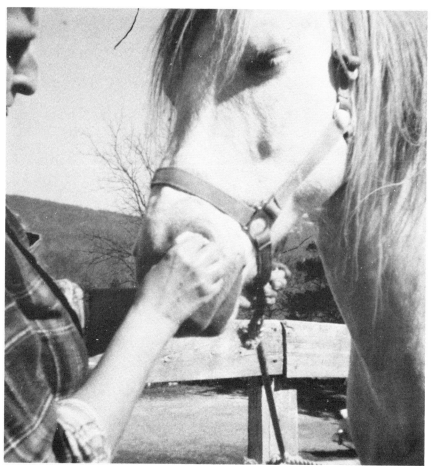

Sponging out of the nostrils removes foreign matter from them.

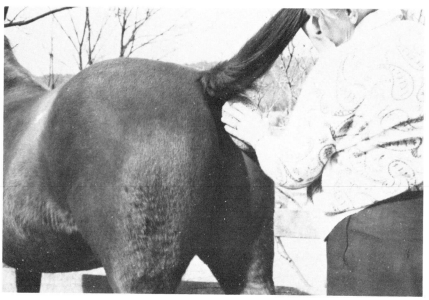

Sponging of the rectum and between the flanks removes dried perspiration and dirt and makes the horse more comfortable.

tail and all around the rectum. Should he seem to have a lot of dry skin or flaky skin around the dock of the tail, apply a bit of baby oil and rub it in well. He will be much more comfortable if you do. Once a week, the sheath of stallions and geldings, and the vulva of mares, are well as their udder, should be washed with warm water and dried. This will remove any foreign matter that has accumulated there and will make the horse a lot more comfortable.

The last step in grooming is to use the stable rubber or piece of natural sheepskin. Taking the linen rubber or sheepskin, begin at the poll and wipe toward the rear of the horse in short, firm strokes. This will produce a high gloss on your horse as it finishes laying the hair flat. The natural lanolin in a piece of sheepskin will produce a higher gloss than will the linen towel, and may be better when used on a horse with a dry coat.

Should your horse need trimming for any reason, whether it be his mane, fetlocks, or his coat, you might want to have a pair of clippers handy. If you do not trim you horse in a hunter clip and only want to keep his fetlocks and mane short, then a pair of hand clippers or roaching shears will be all you need. Hand clippers are small bladed, nonelectric trimmers that are used with much the same action as hand grass shears. You squeeze the handles together and the blades trim the hair off. Fetlock shears are

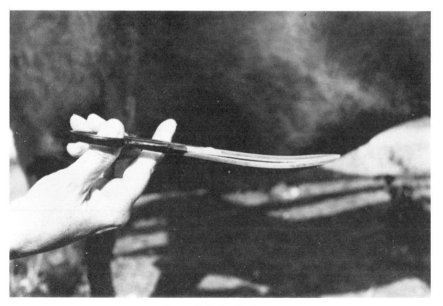

Curved fetlock shears.

designed for trimming the hair around the ankles. The blades of these scissor-like trimmers are curved to fit around the back of the fetlock joint. If you wish to trim the hair of the fetlock, you should take hold of the hair in one hand and, placing the fetlock clippers around the back of the fetlock joint, clip the hair off with the other. Be sure to feel for the ergot at the back of the fetlock. This is a small, horny excresence that protrudes from the center of the back of the fetlock of most horses. It seems to be a remnant of the time when the horse had toes, instead of hoofs. This may be removed by first softening it with baby oil or hoof emmolient and then pulling it free. Though relatively insensitive to pain, it is a good idea to keep the ergots removed, rather than cutting into them with the shears. Though you will not cause pain by cutting the ergots themselves, you might damage or make sore, the root wherefrom they grow should you catch and pull hard on them with the clippers. The ergots of the fetlock are made up of the same substance as are the chestnuts of the legs, and these, too, should be kept soft with baby oil and not allowed to grow to any length. Do not try to cut the dead parts of the chestnuts off with scissors, clippers, or razor blades, as all too many horsemen do. By keeping them soft with oil and gently peeling away the dead material that

The curved blades fit around the back of the pastern for ease of trimming.

forms, you should not need to take the risk of injuring the animal with cutting.

If you want to roach off the mane, that is, cut it level with the neck, the hand clippers are ideal. Beginning, either at the top of the mane or the bottom, whichever you prefer, place the clippers against the base of the mane or the level where the hair grows from the neck and begin to clip, drawing the cut-off hair away from the rest of the mane as you go. If you have a horse with broad withers and you want them to appear more narrow, or if you ride bareback a lot, leave a piece of hair unclipped at the base of the neck. The switch will allow you to hold on, if necessary while riding bareback and will also make the width of the withers seem less. If, on the other hand, you have a narrow withered horse and you want them to look broader, then clip off all of the mane. Unless you have a three-gaited horse or a hunter, you should not trim off the forelock. This is the horse's only protection against flies, and the forelock should really be allowed to grow as long as it will without hanging in the eyes. However, if you are showing your horse in classes that demand the shaved-off forelock, then that too must go.

Roaching of the mane may be done by hand.

Small amounts of hair should be trimmed away at a time.

If you hunt your horse, you will most likely want him trimmed in one of the hunter patterns, both for fashion and for reasons of health on his part. A clipped body will dry much more quickly than will one that is untrimmed. For this, electric clippers are a must, for in most hunter clips, the entire body, save for where the saddle rests and possibly the legs, is shaved and the work is much too slow and tedious for use of hand clippers.

Another aspect of grooming is application of an insect repellant to your horse, particularly in the summer months. Insect repellant for horses comes in several forms, such as spray, bulk liquid, saturated disposable cloths, and stick form. The bulk liquid may either be wiped onto the horse's body with a rag, a mit made especially for the purpose, or may be sprayed on with a sprayer made just for fly repellant. The treated, disposable cloths are nice for local application, such as legs, ears, etc., as is the stick form. The spray or applied liquid is better for over all application. Whatever form you use, be sure to give your horse adequate insect protection all year round.

Good grooming also includes removal of botfly eggs that are laid on the hair of the horse's forelegs. These tiny, yellow, pinhead-sized eggs stick to the hair of the legs, and are often licked off by

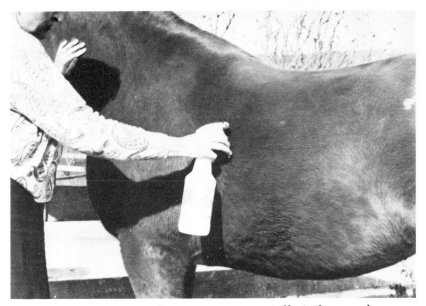

Daily spraying for flies is a must; especially in hot weather.

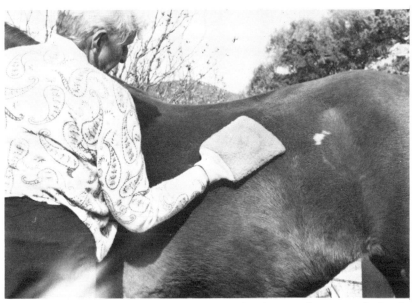

Application of insect repellant may also be done with a terrycloth mit.

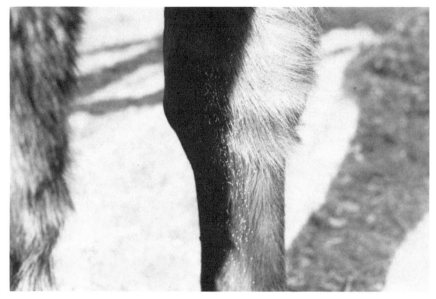

Bot-fly eggs attached to the hair of the horse's legs.

the horse and ingested. They should be removed with a razor blade and then be collected and burned.

Now, what about the grooming of a horse who is trimmed and wears a blanket all the time, or a horse that wears a blanket all of the time because he must keep a nice coat for showing? How does one give a horse like this a thorough grooming, and yet, keep him protected and see that he does not catch cold while the grooming is taking place? The answer to that is fairly simple. You learn to groom the horse without entirely removing the blanket. Now this may sound a bit difficult, but it can be done and quite simply once you get the hang of it. To groom a horse that is blanketed or rugged-up, you first unfasten the front of the blanket or rug and fold it back towards the horse's croup until the fold lies just in the middle of the back. You should now groom the forehand or front of the horse the same as you would, were he not wearing a blanket. After completing the forehand, replace the folded over part and fasten it in place, then turn the rug or blanket forward from the croup toward the withers until the fold clears the line where you ceased the forehand grooming. You should now proceed to groom the hindquarters as you normally would. After having done so, you will replace the rug in its proper position on the horse, seeing

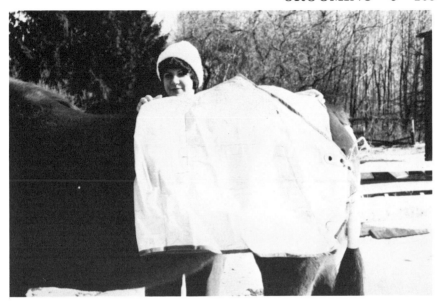

The proper folding back of a blanket for removal from the horse.

that it has not bunched up while folded. After seeing that it is secure and in proper position, you will find that your grooming is complete and the horse was never totally without his covering.

To properly blanket or rug-up a horse, you should place the blanket at the base of the horse's neck, just in front of the withers and unfold it towards his croup, seeing that the hair beneath it lies smooth and flat. After unfolding it, should you find that the rug is too far back on his body, **do not** pull it front, but rather remove the rug and start again, placing it further front on the withers before unfolding it. You should not pull the rug forward as the hair beneath it will be dragged forward also, particularly if the rug is heavy or lined, and when it is finally buckled in place, the horse will be very uncomfortable. After seeing that the rug is in the proper position, you should then fasten the chest straps, bellybands and, if you use one, place the stable roller or surcingle on the animal. A surcingle placed over the rug will help to hold it in place, and the stable roller is designed to fit the horse just behind his withers and is buckled on, like a saddle, to prevent him rolling in his stall. You might also want to wrap or bandage his tail to protect it from being rubbed in the stall. To do this properly you should, after having groomed it thoroughly, begin by placing the

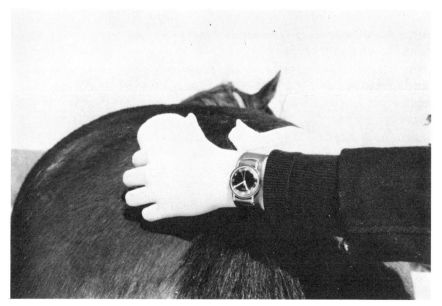

Beginning to wrap the tail.

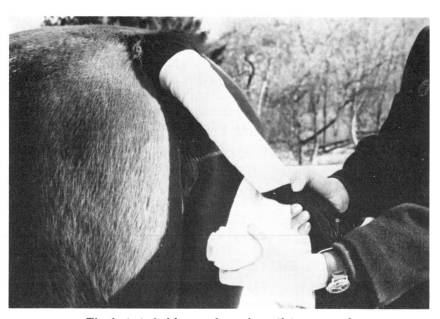

The hair is held smooth as the tail is wrapped.

end of the bandage in the center of the tail at the top on the up, or hair side, or under the tail so that the first free end will lie on the hair side when the wrapping is begun. You should then proceed to wrap the tail, smoothing the hair down as you go, pulling the bandage just tight enough to keep it in place. Wrap the tail downward until you are just a bit beyond the end of the bone where you should begin to wrap back toward the top of the tail again. You will find that the bandage is not long enough to reach the top of the tail again, and this is as it should be. The bandage should be tied off about the middle of the wrapped area, or three-quarters of the way up.

Tying off at the top or dock of the tail may cause injury to the base of the tail, should the horse lean on the knot or otherwise have the knot bruise the flesh of the tail.

Another method of tail wrapping is to begin as you normally would, at the dock of the tail, and proceed to wrap to the proper downward length. Then, if your horse has a long tail and you want to keep it clean, or if you are preparing to breed a mare, you should take the remaining hair and make a loop, lying all of the extra hair upward along the part that was just wrapped. Wrap the hair in with the rest of the hair as you wrap back up along the tail. This keeps the hair clean and out of the way during breeding and in sloppy weather.

A tail properly wrapped.

Tail hair being looped up and wrapped for foul weather.

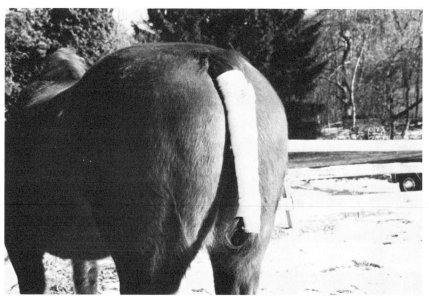

The completed job. Wrapped for bad weather or for breeding.

6
BATHING

I am sure that at one time or another most of us have bathed a dog or washed a car, but one might ask, "how does one undertake the task of washing a horse?" Quite simply — in the same manner that one bathes nearly any other object or animal. The equipment necessary to the task can easily be obtained. Several large buckets or pails, sponges, soap or shampoo and lots of water. If you do not want to get as wet as the horse during the bathing process, you might want to wear a raincoat or riding mac, but do not count on staying dry altogether in any case. The only other thing needed for the bathing is a good, sunny spot where the horse can be tied, and be a willing subject. Now, this last may sound like asking a lot. However, I believe you will soon see that most horses do not object to being bathed, and most even seem to enjoy it quite a bit.

Before you begin to bathe your horse, it might be a good idea for you to brush him down well, especially if he has matted spots of mud or manure anywhere on his coat. This will help to loosen the dirt, making it easier to completely wash it from his coat when bathing him.

If your climate is suitable, it is nice to bathe, or at least, rinse off your horse's back after every ride. However, many parts of the country do not permit this type of cleansing process every day, so I will say this: The best time to give a horse a complete bath is on a good, warm, sunny day, or for most days during the summer months. Most horses can be safely bathed and walked dry without being blanketed in this manner throughout most parts of the country. The best idea for each horse owner, however, is to check with his own veterinarian in his locale as to the best arrangement for bathing his horse.

Now, to begin. Take your horse to the location you have chosen, preferably in full sun, and tie him. If you do not know if your horse has ever been bathed before, it is wise to proceed with caution to avoid startling or frightening him. You should have a number of buckets handy, filled with moderately warm water, and your favorite horse shampoo ready for use. Follow directions on the shampoo bottle. Taking a large sponge, begin applying the warm, soapy water to the horse's body, beginning just behind the ears at the poll. As soon as you know whether or not your horse is going to accept your bathing him, you can briskly begin working the shampoo into a good lather. Continue applying and lathering down both sides of him. Work rather quickly, as horses take cold easily, and should not be allowed to stand around wet any longer than absolutely necessary. Wash the legs and between the flanks well, as sweat and dirt have a tendency to gather and remain there. The mane and tail should also be washed, the tail being dipped directly into the bucket if your horse is not touchy about having his hindquarters handled.

Now that he is washed, take a clean sponge and your rinse water, and beginning at the poll again, begin to rinse your horse. If your horse is used to being bathed, you might want to have

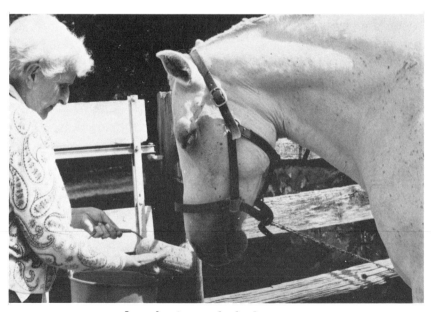

Introduction to the bath sponge.

Shampoo should be placed in the bucket first.

Then warm water added to make suds.

The neck should be wet and soaped first.

Be ready should the horse not be used to baths.

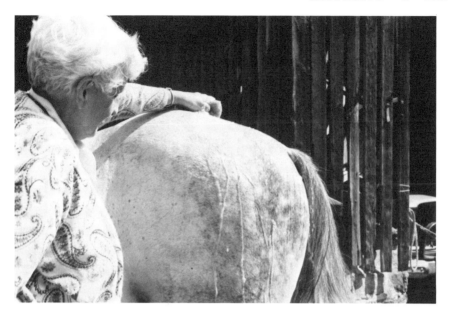

Soap and water should be applied freely if the horse does not resist.

The dock area of the tail should be washed thoroughly.

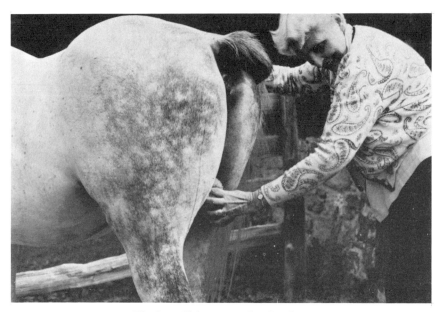

Wash well between the flanks.

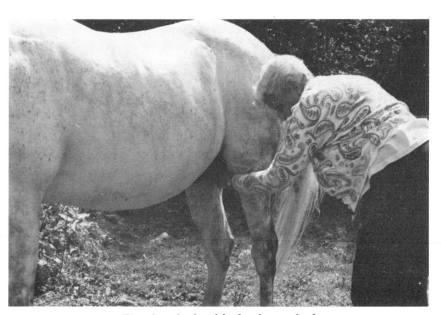

The sheath should also be washed.

Tails may be washed by dipping them directly into the bucket.

someone assist by gently pouring the water down over his neck, *not* his head, but over his neck as you remove the soap with your sponge. You and your assistant should work backward over the whole body in this manner, one pouring and the other wiping as you go. It makes the work go much faster, and it also works well if you can both work this way during the washing procedure. It is a good idea to rinse the horse several times, especially the mane and tail, as any dried soap or shampoo is going to make the horse itch, and soap that has dried in the mane and tail may cause dandruff. When you are finished, feel your horse's coat. You may be surprised to feel that it is full of grit. If this is the case, it is a good idea to resoap, rewash, and rerinse. Many horses that cannot be bathed regularly pick up a great amount of dirt and grit in their coats, and sometimes daily brushing cannot eliminate all of it. It is best, therefore, when you bathe the horse, to see that his coat is as clean as possible after each bathing.

After the final rinse, you and your assistant should take a clean sweat scraper and draw off all the water possible from his coat. The sweat scraper acts like a "squeegee" and squeezes water from the horse's coat as it is run across his body. When no more water can be removed from the horse, it is time to walk him. Do this just as you would if he were hot and sweating from a ride. If he will lunge, then lunge him at a walk, but do it until he is perfectly dry. As he dries, you will begin to see dark patches on his coat that are still holding water. Now and then you may want to take your sweat scraper and go over these spots. Sometimes you will be able to remove more water gathered in these wet spots. If there is any air moving, such as a light breeze, you might want to drape a dry towel across the animal's back and loins as he walks, to help soak up the remaining water. It is also a good idea to rub the horse all over with a large beach towel or two after you have used the sweat scraper and before you walk him. This will aid in removing a great deal of water from his coat.

The hair of the tail should be squeezed out, just as you would squeeze water out of your own hair, and after you have squeezed out as much water as you possibly can, you might find it advisable to tie a towel around the tail in order to soak up more water while the horse is walking. The towel may be removed before the horse is perfectly dry so that the hair does not dry in mats.

After the horse is perfectly dry, his face should be sponged off with clean water and dried with a towel. The head itself should

A dry towel may be placed over the horse's back to aid in soaking up excess water after the bath.

never be soaked, or if at all possible, soaped. The feet and ankles, too, should again be rinsed, as they probably have picked up a lot of grit in the wet hair, and should be patted or pressed dry with a clean towel. They should not be rubbed hard to dry them.

Most horsemen find that after a while, it is a good idea to have two sets of brushes for their horses. One set is kept clean and one set is used. After a bath, the clean set should be brought out and used, while the set that was formerly used should be washed well, allowed to dry, and be put away for use after the next bath. This way, your horse always has a clean set of brushes for use on his clean coat. There is no sense in brushing a perfectly clean horse with dirty, gritty brushes.

Now that the horse is dry, he should be brushed well to ensure that his hair is placed in the proper pattern, both for looks and for his comfort. Also, brushing after a bath stimulates the oil glands in his skin and begins to add luster to his coat again. Shine in a horse's coat is produced by an accumulation of oil in the hair, and washing removes the oil. Now, too, his mane and tail should be thoroughly combed. A horse's mane and tail should never be allowed to dry in ropes, knots, or mats, and by now, the mane and tail will have ceased to drip, but will not be completely dried. Combing a wet mane and tail is not easy, but it beats having to roach the mane and trim the tail in order to remove knotted, unremovable dried mats.

If you wish to roach your horse's mane, that is, clip it off against the neck, as is the custom with some styles of riding, then do so before the horse is bathed. It makes it much easier to wash away tiny bits of hair that otherwise might cling to the horse's skin along the line of the mane, and thus, irritate him for days afterward. Too, any clipping of the body or tail that is to be done, should be done before the bath is given for the same reason. Also, it is dangerous to use an electric clipper on a horse's wet body because of the possibility of shock to both horse and groom. Pasterns should also be trimmed before the bath is given, thus minimizing the time that the ankle joints are kept wet during the bath, and cutting down on the amount of dirt collected in the wet hair while being walked dry.

After the mane and tail have dried, if they seem a bit unruly or dull, a small amount of baby oil, worked into the roots of both mane and tail, and combed through the hair, will do wonders in a matter of minutes, just as in regular grooming. The oil slicks the hair, removes dryness caused by the washing, and adds shine.

After the bath, be sure the feet are clean and dry, with no wetness remaining in the clefts of the frog or around the ankles and heels. The horse should now be allowed some time to sun himself at liberty. And do not be surprised or angry if the first thing he does is roll around in the dirt.

7
FOOT CARE

One of the most important parts of good horse care is proper care of the hoofs. Like the old adage says, "no foot, no horse," and it is true. A horse is only as good as his feet, so the feet should be given proper attention and care to help the horse stay at his best. Basically, the hoof is composed of a horny material that contains the bones and laminae of the foot. The foot is composed of the crust or wall, the coronary ring and band, the bars, the laminae the sole,and the frog. The crust or wall of the hoof is the portion that is seen when the foot is placed on the ground, and reaches from the termination of the hair of the leg to the ground. The front part of the hoof, the toe, is the deepest, being about three inches in height, and becoming shallower at the sides, known as the quarters, and the smallest at the back part of the hoof. The rear or heels of the hoof being about an inch to an inch and a half in height. The crust is composed of numerous horny fibers connected together by an elastic membranous substance, and it extends from the coronet to the base of the hoof. It differs materially in its texture, its elasticity, its growth, and its occasional brittleness according to the state wherein it is kept. The outside of the hoof should be smooth and level. Protuberances, rings around the crust, depressions, or hollows, all may indicate that there is some type of internal disturbance in the hoof.

The thickness of the crust, in the front of the foot, is rather more than half an inch, and it becomes gradually thinner towards the quarters and heels, but this often varies to a considerable extent. In some hoofs, it is not more than half the above thickness. Horses with very thin walls are often difficult to shoe and may be injured quite readily in the process. Often a horse that has been injured in shoeing will be difficult to manage in subsequent shoeing attempts.

While the crust becomes thinner towards both quarters, it is more so at the inner quarter than at the outer, because more weight is thrown upon it than the outer. This is because it is more under the horse. The elasticity of the inner quarter is called into play more than the elasticity of the outer quarter, and this flexing helps to prevent injury. However, when the quarters of the hoof are held in one place, such as by shoeing, and the elasticity is diminished, the inner quarter will suffer the most. Here, it is most often that corns are seen, where contraction often starts, and where most sand cracks are found. Because of the inner quarter being thinner and more flexible than the outer quarter, the inner heel is often found to wear faster, due to the weight taken on it. Good trimming by the blacksmith will keep the heels level and sound.

The coronet or coronary ring: The crust does not vary much in thickness until it nears the top of the foot where it thins out quickly. Internally, it is scoop-shaped or hollowed-out. It also changes its color and texture, and seems nearly like a continuation of the skin of the leg, however, this is not so. This upper, thin part of the hoof is called the coronary ring. It extends around the upper portion of the hoof and receives within it, or covers, a thickened extension of the skin called the coronary ligament. This ligament is thickly supplied with blood vessels, and many of these help produce the crust itself. That is why when the coronary band is injured, such as with a sand crack or quittor, it takes so long for the hoof to regrow. If the coronary band is badly damaged, a permanent scar of the hoof may result and the blood vessels in the band will be deformed or disfigured and produce deformed hoof crust.

The bars: At the back of the foot, the wall of the hoof, instead of continuing around and forming a circle, is suddenly bent in to form the heel. The bars are, in fact, a continuation of the crust, forming an acute angle and meeting at a point at the tip of the frog. The inside of the bars, like the inside of the crust, presents a continuation of the horny ridges or leaves, showing that it is a part of the same substance. The bars are very important. The arch, which bars form on either side, between the frog and the quarters, is contrived to both permit and to limit the expansion of the foot. When the foot is placed on the ground, the weight of the horse is thrown on the leaves of the inside of the bars. The arches then shorten and widen, in order to permit the expansion of the quarters. Conversely, when the horse raises the foot, the bars lengthen and become narrow, and thus, bring the foot back to is original shape. The bars also give security and stability to the frog, and should never be trimmed or touched by the blacksmith.

The leaves: The inside crust of the hoof is covered by thin, horny leaves extending all around it, and reaching from the coronary ring to the toe. They are about five hundred in number, broadest at their base, and terminating in the most delicate expansion of horn. They resemble the underside of a mushroom or toadstool. In the front they run in a direction from the coronet to the toe, and towards the quarters they slant more from front to back. They are quite elastic and really support most of the weight of the horse.

The sole: This is the underside of the foot and occupies the greater portion of the concave and elastic surface of the foot, extending from the crust to the bars of the frog. The sole is not as thick as the crust, as it does not support as much weight as the crust and because it is intended to expand in order to prevent concussion when the horse's weight is thrown upon it. It is not as brittle as the crust and is more elastic. The sole is thickest at the toe because this is where the first and principal stress is thrown upon it. It is also thicker where it unites with the crust than towards the center, for a similar and evident reason; because there, the weight is first thrown and takes the greatest amount of stress. In nature it is, to a certain degree, hollow, and the reason for this is simple. The sole is intended to descend or yield somewhat with the weight of the horse, and by doing so, lessen the shock to the bones and tendons that would result during violent or fast action, or exercise. This type of shock absorption and cushioning can only be given by a hollow sole. A sole that is flat, that is, one that touches the ground, cannot be brought lower, and the frog cannot do its work properly, that is, to hold the foot securely to the ground. When shoeing a horse, the blacksmith should be sure that the shoe does not in any way interfere with the sole, nor partially cover it, as this will prevent the natural lowering action of the sole. If the sole is held up by faulty shoeing, the coffin bones inside the hoof will bump against the inside of the sole and cause lameness. Stones that wedge themselves between the shoe and the sole of the foot cause great lameness, as this causes the sole not to bend or yield as it should.

The frog: In the space between the bars is the frog. It is a triangular portion of horn, projecting from the sole, almost on a level with the crust, and covering and defending a soft and elastic substance, called the sensible frog. Its shape is familiar to most horsemen. It is firmly attached to, or united with the sole, but is perfectly distinct from it. It is softer and far more elastic. It comes in contact with the ground and prevents the horse from slipping, particularly in galloping, where the heel comes in contact with the ground first. It aids mainly in the expansion of the foot. In order to function properly, it must come in contact with the ground, and in unshod horses does so naturally. The practice of cutting the frog back when shoeing, is detrimental to the horse and highly unnecessary. Only ragged pieces of frog should be trimmed back. When trimming, the ragged or detached parts should be cut away to bring the frog just above or within the level of the shoe. It will then, in the descent of the sole, press against the ground and take up the shock. Shoeing helps protect the frog from undue wear, tear, and bruising that it would get when the horse is used daily and/or worked hard. Shoeing in this way helps to protect the frog, sole, and wall, yet allows the frog to do its work properly.

The pedal bone: The inside of the hoof should now be studied to some degree. The lower pastern is partly contained in the hoof and attached to it, and fully enclosed inside the hoof is the pedal bone. It is fitted to and fills the fore part of the hoof, occupying about half of it. It is of light and spongy structure, and is filled with minute foramina (holes or pores). Through these, the blood vessels and nerves of the foot pass. These nerves and blood vessels are protected by the bone, and allow free circulation of blood and nerve impulses to the foot at all times. The porosity of the bone allows free circulation, yet, protects and supports all of the nerves and blood vessels that would otherwise be crushed with the horse's weight, if it were allowed to press in upon them.

On the front and side of the pedal bone are laminae — cartilaginous fleshy plates — running down between the horny leaves of the crust. The substance that connects these laminae with the pedal bone is highly elastic, and necessarily so, for when the horse is at rest his whole weight is supported by them. These laminae are what yield and allow the pedal bone to flex downward toward the sole when the horse is in motion. These, too, are the laminae that break down and separate during an attack of founder or laminitis. In doing so, they allow the bone to drop down toward the sole, and depending upon the severity of the attack, their separation from each other or from the bone itself may permanently cripple the horse.

The sensible sole: Between the pedal bone and the horny outer sole is the sensible sole, or the quick or live, fleshy part of the sole. This is formed of a substance of a ligamentous or tendinous nature, and beneath that a cutical, or skin-like layer, which is richly supplied with blood vessels. It also aids in shock absorption and assists in the formation of the horny part of the sole. Leaving a space for the frog, it covers the bars and is united with the wall of the hoof with some laminae. It is here, where it is thickest. It is the sensible sole that causes lameness when inflammed by pressures such as those of wedged stones, corns, etc.

The sensible frog: The forepart of the hoof is filled by the pedal bone, and the rear part by the sensible frog. This is a soft mass, partly ligamentous and partly tendinous. Its shape corresponds to the remaining part of the inner hoof cavity. The forepart is attached to the rear of the pedal bone and farther back it adheres to the lower part of the cartilages of the heels, and here it begins to form the rounded protuberances that form the heel of the hoof or foot. It occupies the whole back part of the foot above the horny frog. Running immediately above the frog and along the greater part of it is the *perforans flexor* tendon, wich passes over the navicular bone and is inserted into the heel of the pedal bone.

The navicular bone: This is placed behind and beneath the lower pastern bone, and behind and above the pedal bone, and thus, forms a joint with both bones. It strengthens these two bones and receives much of the weight that is thrown upon the lower pastern. The navicular bone helps to support the flexor tendon, and without it, the tendon would gradually be crushed by the constant weight of the horse. In navicular disease, the navicular bone deteriorates and somewhat allows the weight of the horse to settle upon the tendon. In some cases, the tendon becomes adhered to the bone, lessening the tendon's efficiency, and often necessitates the horse being put away. The whole of the inside of the foot is supported by a series of cartilages. These cartilages support the pedal bone, the navicular bone, and both sides of the frog, thus giving added support to the whole internal structure of the foot.

Now, what about proper foot care? Horses should be shod when worked constantly to prevent the rapid wearing of the hoofs, and also to protect the hoofs from bruises and foreign objects. However, horses that are not working, or horses that are being used for breeding purposes, need not be shod. Shoeing should be done only by a qualified blacksmith and should be done on a regularly scheduled basis. The usual schedule is a trim and a reset every six to eight weeks, however, this may vary according to how much or how little your horse's feet grow. Some may require attention in four to six weeks, while others may go up to ten weeks without a reset. Daily hoof care is a must for healthy, sound feet. The hoofs should be picked out twice a day, morning and night, and shoes checked for loose nails, foreign objects caught in them, or lodged beneath them, and for secure attachment to the hoof. Unshod feet should be checked for broken walls, splits or cracks, and bruised soles. Attention should also be paid to the moisture of the hoof. Hoofs that are too dry often shell off around the front of the wall, or become brittle and crack off in quite large pieces. Special preparations for hoof dryness are available at tack shops and some feed mills. Daily application of a hoof dressing will help to restore the necessary moisture to the hoof and will aid in preventing further drying of the hoof. Hoofs should also be examined when they are picked out to see that the feet are not being kept too damp, and that thrush is not developing. Thrush is a fungus infection of the frog of the foot and is caused mainly by standing a horse in a dirty stall, or in a stall that is not kept clean and dry enough. Some horses seem to be more prone to contracting thrush than others, and while the fungus is easy to treat in the early stages, it can become quite severe if left untreated.

One of the first signs of thrush is an offensive-smelling discharge given off by the frog. The skin of the frog will be blackened looking, and may begin peeling off when the foot is picked out. The frog may or may not be sensitive, depending upon how far the problem has developed, and upon your particular horse. Advanced thrush usually progresses inward into the frog and may begin to destroy the inner sensitive frog, and in extreme cases, the bones themselves. If thrush is found to be present in the hoof, thrush remedies are available at tack shops, and treatment is quite simple. The medicine may either be applied directly to the frog, or a cotton pad may be saturated with the medicine, and when the hoof has been cleaned, the pad will be pressed into the cleft of the frog securely and allowed to remain there until the next cleaning of the hoof. The pad should be changed at each hoof cleaning and the treatment continued until the problem clears up. In the early stages, this should clear up in about a week. The horse may be used normally as long as he is not lame. When being used, the cotton pad should be removed, so that it does not rub or chafe the frog, but should be replaced when the horse is not being used, or after the ride.

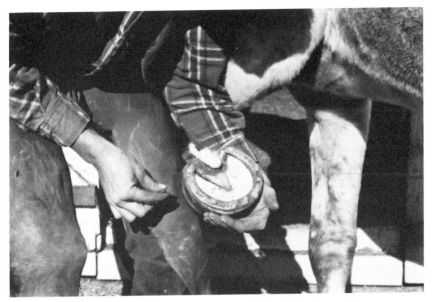

Thrush may be treated by packing the cleft of the frog with cotton.

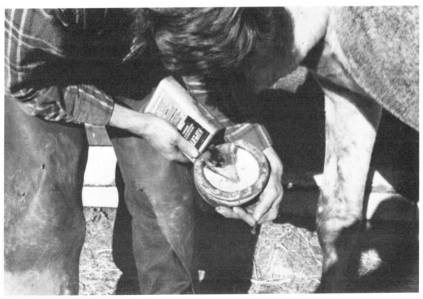

Apply thrush dressing directly to the cotton that is in the cleft of the frog.

As mentioned before, only a qualified blacksmith should be allowed to trim or shoe your horse, but it is nice to know just what steps the smith will take in preparing both the horse's hoof, and the shoes for application to the hoofs. If the horse is shod, the first thing the blacksmith or farrier (as he is properly known) does, is to remove the shoes that are presently on the horse. To do this, he will unclinch the ends of the nails that will be seen on the fronts and sides of the horse's hoof when the horse is standing in normal position. To do this, he will use a hammer and clinch cutter. The clinch cutter is placed under the crimped down nails ends and is struck upwards against them with the hammer. This unbends the turned down nail ends and makes it possible for him to remove the shoe without to much pull to the horse's hoofs. These clinched over nail ends hold the shoe securely to the hoof. Next, he will hold the horse's hoof in the same position used to clean out the hoofs, only the hoof will be placed between his knees so that he can hold the foot securely, yet have both hands to work with. He will now take a tool called a pincer, and taking hold of the shoe along one quarter, will proceed to loosen the shoe by pulling outward from the hoof. He will do this all along the shoe, moving from one side, to the toe, around to the other side, or in whatever

A hoof before it is trimmed and the shoe reset.

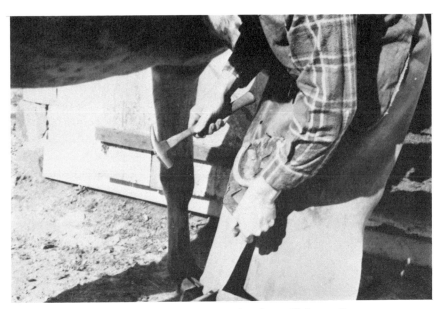

The farrier cutting the clinches off the nails.

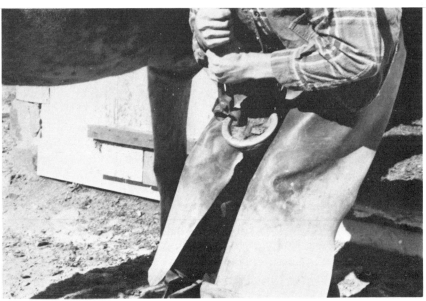

Using the pincers to loosen the shoe.

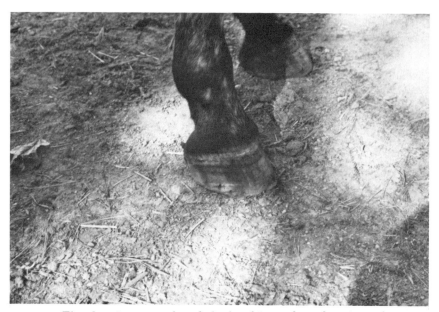

The shoe is removed and the hoof is ready to be trimmed.

pattern happens to work best for him. The now loose shoe will be pulled off, the nails coming with it. Nails should be examined after the removal of the shoe to see that they are, first, all accounted for, and secondly, to see that they are all nearly the same length, and that none of the nail has broken off and remained in the nail hole of the foot, or that it has not broken off into the foot itself. Do not be hesitant about asking your blacksmith to check for this if he does not do it himself. Better to ask and be safe, than sorry. The next step is the trimming of the hoof. To do this, the farrier will use a tool called a hoof cutter. This tool is shaped much like the pincer, however, where pincers blades are dull on both edges, the hoof cutter will be sharp, either on one blade or both. The farrier will now proceed to cut away the proper amount of hoof so that the foot is shortened to the required length. Again, he will begin on one quarter and proceed around to the other side of the foot in a circular pattern. The piece of hoof that he trims away will probably be all in one piece when it has been removed from the foot. You will be able to see clearly the holes left by the nails of the just removed shoe in the piece of cut away hoof.

Next the farrier will use a tool called a draw knife. This is a small, curved blade, set in a wooden handle, and the edge of the

This is the way the foot will look when in need of a trim.

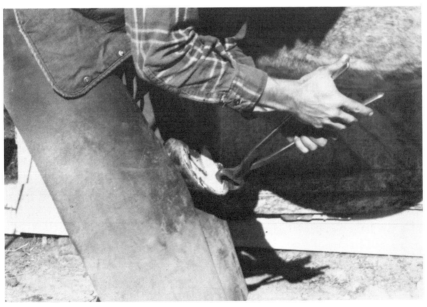

Beginning to trim the hoof with the hoof cutters.

This is what the piece of hoof will look like when it has been removed from the foot. Notice the nail holes in it.

blade is hooked around in a semicircle. With the knife, the farrier will trim away all of the dead skin of the sole and frog. The name draw knife is used, as this type of knife was often used to draw out or withdraw stones lodged in the hoof, and also to cut or draw out corns in the foot.

After the foot has been trimmed out, the farrier will now use a rasp and file the foot to a level, so that the horse will stand with his feet even, and to present a level surface where to attach the shoe. The rasp should only be used on the flat or striking surface of the foot, except for a brief use to smooth out the edges around the toe, and should never be used to thin out the hoof walls.

The farrier will now check the shoe to see where and how badly it is worn. If the wear is greatly uneven, he will recommend a new set of shoes. If the shoe can be reused he will now reshape the shoe, so that it will fit the newly trimmed hoof. Be sure that your farrier shapes the shoe to fit the foot, and does not trim the foot to fit the shoe. An exception to this may be in corrective shoeing where many times unusual procedures are necessary in order to cure a particular foot problem. However, this is an exception, rather than the rule. To reshape the shoe, the farrier will heat the

Using the draw knife to cut away dead and ragged hoof tissue.

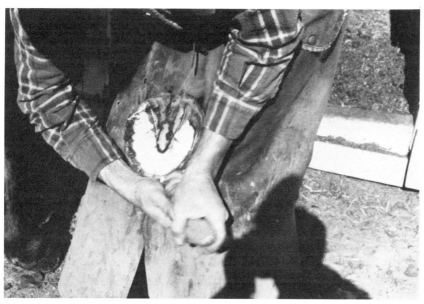

Notice how white and clean the sole is after the dead material has been removed.

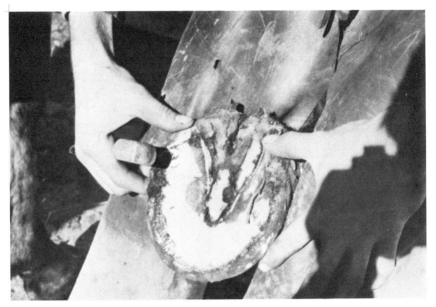

The sole and frog free from dead tissues.

The rasp is used to make the foot level.

The rasp is used from heel to toe.

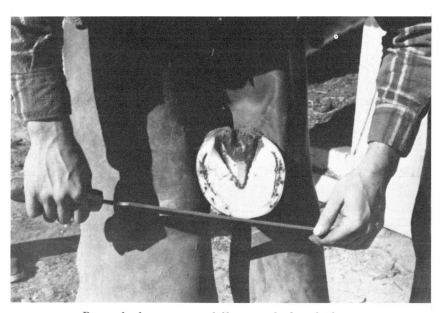

Ragged edges are carefully smoothed with the rasp.

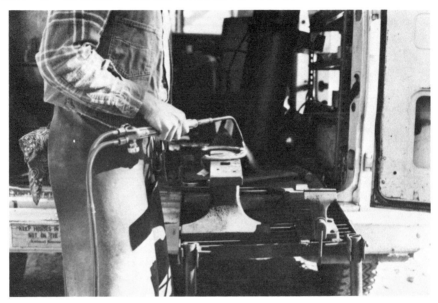

Acetylene torches are often used to heat the shoes.

part that must be bent, and to do this, he will either use an ascetylene torch or build a fire in a small stove that he may carry with him in his truck. Once the shoe has been properly heated, and shoes will glow quite red when ready for reshaping, he will procede to hammer the shoe into the proper roundness or levelness that is suited to your horse's hoof. Shoes should always be heated to be reshaped and never hammered cold. Cold bending of iron causes the metal to lose its temper or resiliancy, and may cause it to break under stress.

Once the farrier has shaped the shoe to where he thinks it will fit the horse's hoof, he will cool it somewhat by dipping the shoe into a bucket of cold water. In most cases, the farrier will place a nail punch in one of the nail holes in the shoe and use this as a handle to hold the shoe for further fitting. In most cases, the farrier will now take the somewhat cooled shoe and place it lightly against the hoof in the position it will be when nailed on. The heat from the shoe will sear or mark wherever it touches the hoof, and thus, the farrier will be able to see where the shoe needs to be further bent and at what angle or degree. This touching of the shoe to the hoof while the shoe is still fairly hot does not cause the horse any pain. The walls of the hoof are insensitive to pain, as are your

The heated metal is then pounded into the proper shape by hand.

The shoe is shaped to the structure of the horse's hoof.

The shoe is cooled in water to temper the metal.

Nail holes are punched out with a tool designed just for the purpose.

The semi-hot shoe is touched to the prepared hoof to mark it so that the farrier can see where adjustments in fit need to be made.

fingernails or hair, thus, they can be trimmed and singed with little notice by the animal.

Once the shoes have been properly shaped, they are now ready to have borium applied, if needed. This is a substance that is welded to the shoes in spots to prevent slipping when the horse is ridden on macadam or other hard surfaces. If the horse is ridden mainly on trails or in meadows, borium will not be needed. The farrier can recommend whether or not it is needed.

Now the shoe is ready to be nailed onto the foot. Again, the hoof will be placed between the farrier's knees, and the soles of the foot should be brushed off with the hand to see that no small stones, etc. have been picked up while the horse was waiting for his shoe. The shoe will now be placed in position and will be given one more check for fit, then the nails will be placed in the nail slots in the shoe and driven into the hoof. Shoeing nails are slightly curved in the shank and this is done for a very important reason. If the shanks of the nails were straight, there is a good chance that they would not come out through the hoof crust again so that they could be bent over and clinched down. There is also the chance that they would penetrate the quick or sensitive membranes of the

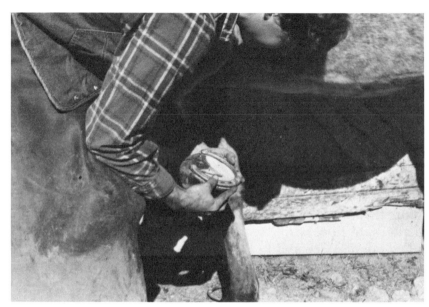

The prepared shoe is rechecked for fit.

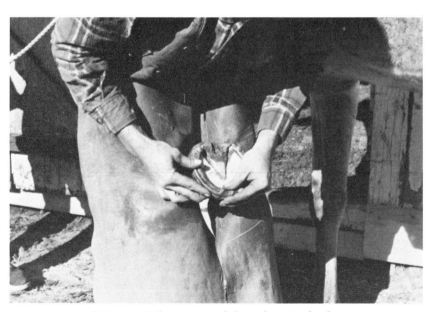

It is carefully examined from front to back.

hoof and cause lameness. Straight shanked nails would go straight up inside the wall of the hoof, however, the curving of the nail shanks ensures that the nails do indeed, come back out on the outside of the hoof, and this enables the farrier to complete his work. The nails should be placed in such a way that the shanks reappear at about the same angle and on a curving line with one another. Unless for a specific reason, see that the farrier does not place the nails extremely high in the walls of the hoofs, as the higher nails are placed, the easier it is for him to prick the horse, as the wall becomes narrower the further up inside the hoof it goes. Each nail shank will be bent over as it is finished with, and before the farrier goes onto the next nail. Nails should be applied on alternate sides with each nail. This keeps the shoe from being pulled out of place and keeps one side from being drawn tighter than the other.

Once all of the nails have been driven in and the shanks bent over, the next step is to cut the shanks off and clinch or block the nails. This is done by taking the shank of the nail in the small slit in the tail of the hammer and giving it a twist around to seat it, and then by cutting off the remaining length of shank with a pair of

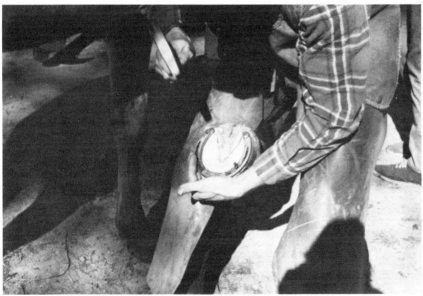

The first of the nails is now driven into the hoof.

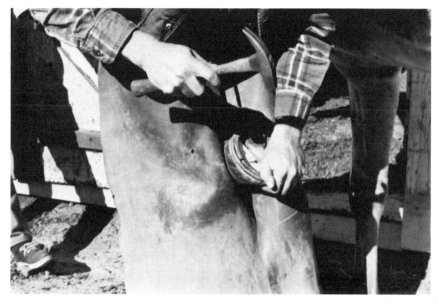

Nails are placed in alternate sides of the hoof so that the shoe is not pulled out of place.

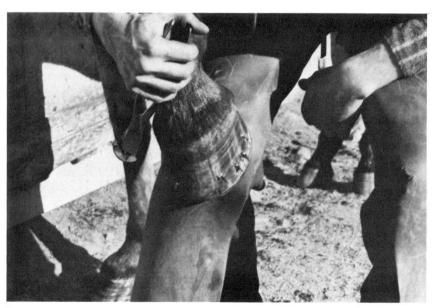

The shanks of the nails are then bent down against the outside of the hoof.

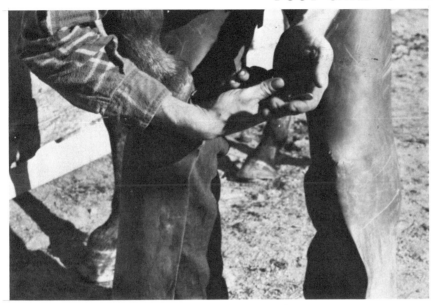

They are then twisted around and clipped off.

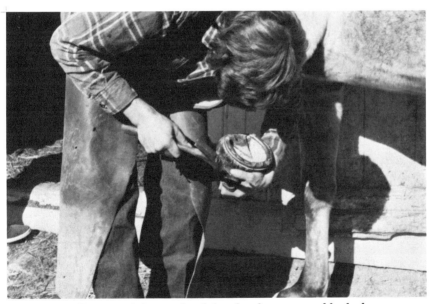

The remaining ends of the shanks are now blocked.

The edges of the shanks are filed smooth.

clippers. When all of the shanks have been removed, the side of the rasp will be used to file the sharp edges of the protruding shank stumps to smoothness. A block, a small square of metal, will now be placed against the nails heads on the striking surface of the shoe, and the farrier will proceed to hammer flat the remaining shank stumps to the outside of the hoof. This blocking keeps the nails from being loosened or driven back out of the foot when the shanks are flattened against the sides of the hoofs.

A tool called a clincher will now be used. This pincerlike tool has one upcurved jaw, and it is placed with one jaw against the nailhead on the striking suface of the shoe, and the curved jaw is placed up the front of the shoe or hoof, against the remaining end of the clipped nail shank. The clincher is then squeezed to further fasten the nail into the hoof, and finally, the shank is given a sharp rap with a hammer to make sure it will not loosen.

The edges of the hoof that meet the shoe will now be filed level, smooth and even with the edges of the shoe so that they do not break off or catch on things because of roughness. The job is now complete.

The same procedure is used on all four hoofs and will vary only in cases of corrective shoeing or with a troublesome horse. Should

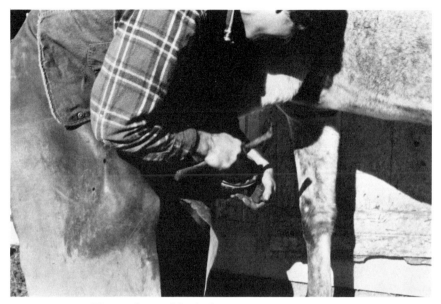

The nails are blocked again if any seem loose.

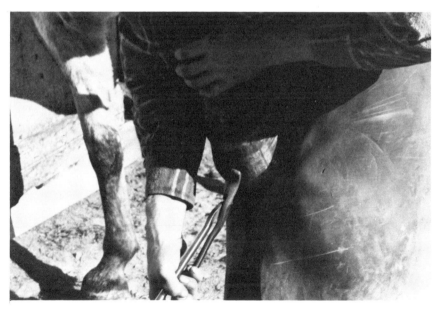

The clincher is now used to press the shanks completely flat.

Additional flattening of the shanks may be done directly with the hammer.

The front edges of the hoof are filed off flush with the shoe.

Smoothing the edges is of great importance. It lessens the chance of rough pieces of hoof catching and breaking off.

The finished result.

your horse show signs of lameness in the day or two following shoeing, do not hesitate to alert your farrier. Most professional farriers rarely prick a horse, but now and then, often due to a slight variation inside the horse's hoof, it may happen. The horse may become lame. Lameness from a prick or nail pressure can easily be made better by having the farrier remove the offending nail. He will be able to tell what nail is causing the trouble by tapping on all of the nails with a hammer. The offending nail will cause the horse to flinch when it is struck and this is a telltale sign of pressure or nail prick.

Horseshoes come in a variety of designs, each with a specific purpose in the design. One of the most common things seen in shoes is fullering. Fullering is a groove on the striking surface of the shoe wherein the nail holes are punched. This fullering groove allows the nailheads to be driven flush with the striking surface, and thus, lessens the chance of speedy cut caused by overreach. Another fairly common design, along with the fullering, is seating out of a shoe. This is a beveling of the inner striking surface, and it lightens the weight of the shoe.

Other variations include spreader bars for contracted heels, toe cleats for plow horses, trailer heels for overreach and splay feet, turned heels to raise them, and toe clips and side clips for a more firm attachment of shoe to hoof. There are also toe covers or tips for when the horse is turned out to grass unshod, and the toes need protection. There are also lightweight, aluminum shoes for racehorses.

Regardless of what type shoe your horse needs, his feet should be well taken care of so that he can do and feel his best. One of the most commonly seen foot problems in shod hoofs is the edges of the hoof breaking off around the edges of the shoe, and this is caused by the shoes being left on the foot for too long a period of time between resets. Regularity in shoeing and trimming schedules is a must if the feet are to be properly kept. The longer hoofs of the show horses such as Tennessee Walkers and Saddlebreds need even more diligent care, due to the unnatural length and because of pads and blocks used under the hoofs that cause them to grow to the desired angle, and to be sure that strains and sprains do not occur because of the hoof's abnormal lengths.

If a horse is to remain unshod, then a trim and hoof examination is still a regular necessity to keep his feet in the best condition. Horses, too, are plagued with foot troubles as is man, and they are prone to corns, bruises, and even blisters if the shoe is too long and rubs against the bulb of the heels. Bruise treatment is best discussed with your vet, corns usually need to be cut out, either by the farrier or by the vet. Blisters can be cured by removing the shoe and doctoring the blister. However, good hoof care and attention to begin with can lessen greatly the chance of the above happening to your horse. (For further discussion of foot troubles see the illness chapter.)

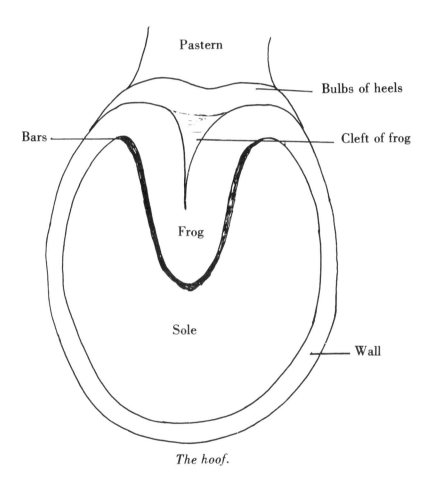

The hoof.

Internal hoof structure.

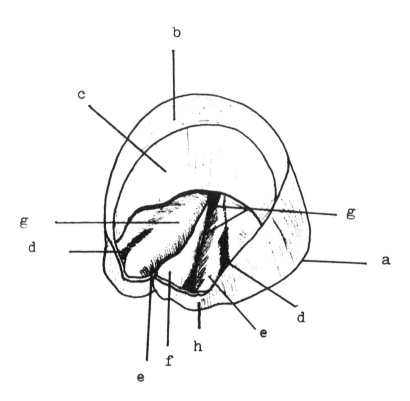

a– *The external crust seen at the quarter.*
b– *The coronary ring.*
c– *Small horny plates that line the crust.*
d– *The same continued over the bars.*
e– *The two concave surfaces of the inside of the horny frog.*
f– *The external cleft of the frog.*
g– *The bars.*
h– *The rounded part of the heels, belonging to the frog.*

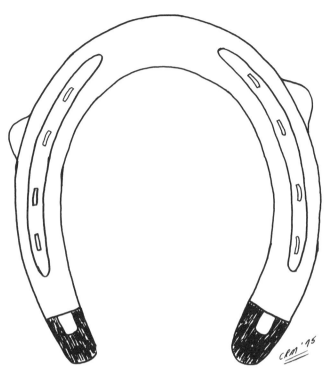

Shoe with side clips and rolled heels.

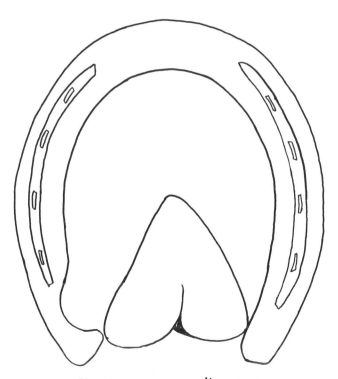

Shoe is cut away to relieve corn.

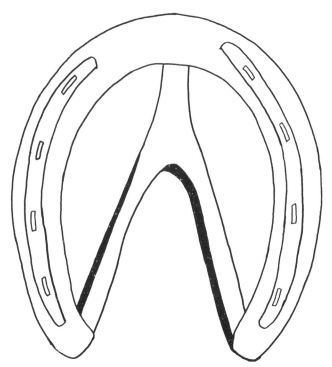

Shoe with spreader spring – to cure contracted heels.

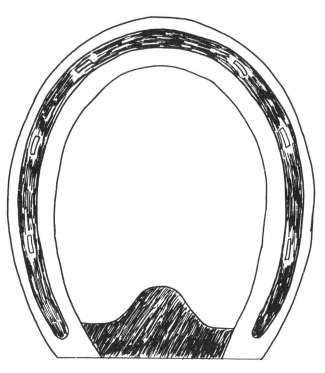

Bar Shoe for support of weak heels.

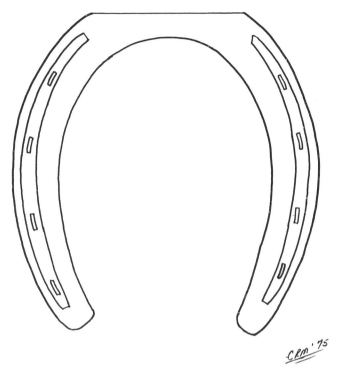

Square or cut off toe to cure or correct overreach.

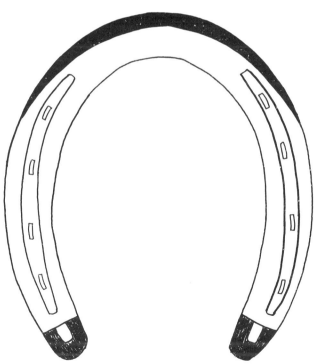

Rolled toe for foundered foot or to cure stumbling. Turned heels.

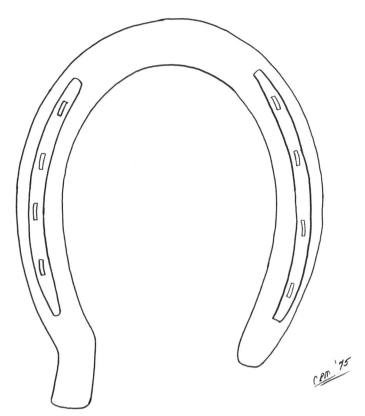

Shoe with trailer heel — may be on either heel of shoe — to cure forging and/or splayed feet.

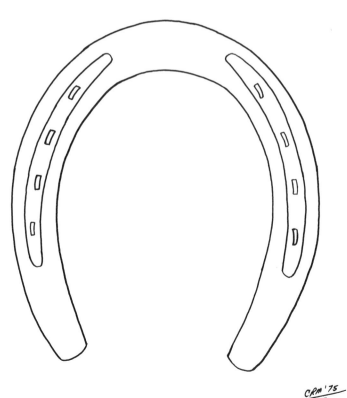

Plain fullered shoe.

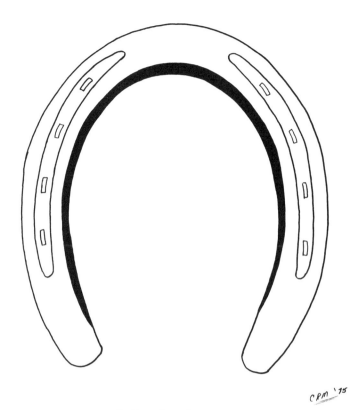

Fullered and seat out.

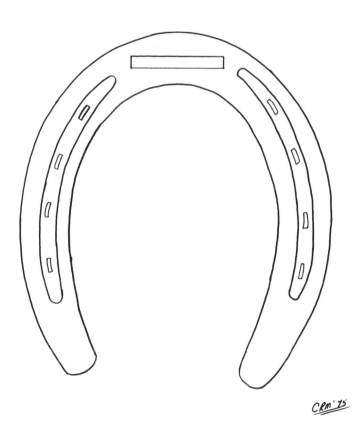

Toe bar cleat for use of carriage horse.

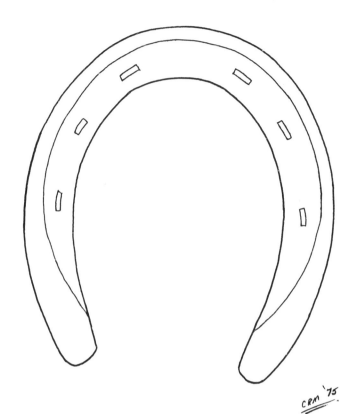

Concave shoe for extra light weight.

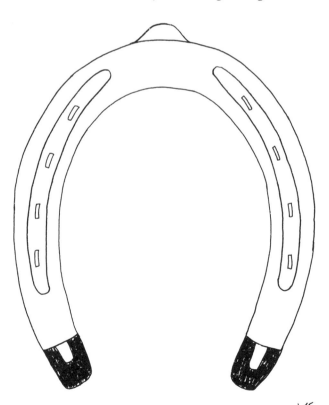

Turned heel and toe clip.

8
TEETH

Most horsemen know how to tell a horse's age by his teeth, at least with a fair degree of accuracy up to the age of nine years. More experienced horsemen are able to determine a horse's age as far as twenty years, though not with as much accuracy. But, what of the novice? How does he determine how old a horse is? And does the novice even know how many teeth a horse has? Most novices only know that a horse has teeth, big teeth, and that he does not want to get too close to them. The real novice might not even know that the horse has a space between his incisors and the back grinding molars that enables him to hold a bit in his mouth, let alone determine his age by his teeth.

Like anything else, learning to determine the age of a horse by his teeth takes time and must be learned by doing. Even here, practice makes perfect or nearly so.

To begin with, let us look at one individual tooth. A horse's teeth are not like human teeth. There is no central nerve running up into the tooth, therefore, the horse feels little or no pain and has very little sensation in his teeth at all. Also, a horse's teeth are not made up structurally like a human's teeth. A horse's teeth are made up of enamel, a cementing substance, a bony ivory, running in shafts the length of the tooth. As the teeth are ground down in the process of eating, new bone or ivory comes to bear from the inside of the tooth, thus, always presenting a hard, firm, true grinding surface to the food. A horse's teeth also never stop growing. The tooth of a horse is in a constant state of growth and may sometimes need to be filed down, should he begin to bite or cut up the inside of his face when he feeds. This filing down of the teeth is called *floating* and can be done by most veterinarians.

As the tooth wears down, new bony material and cementing surfaces are constantly being raised to the surface of the tooth, thus, keeping the tooth in constant growth. This pattern of cement and bone permits full use of the teeth as instruments of food processing, well into advanced age, and if the horse is well cared for, and has his teeth checked yearly, the teeth will serve him well until his death.

New teeth are entirely covered with enamel, as are human teeth, however, the enamel of a horse's tooth dips down deeply into each pocket of the tooth. As the enamel is worn off, the center of each tooth becomes level on the biting surface and the corresponding "black mark" therein is eliminated. Though a worn down tooth is said to be unmarked, it will not be pure white. The grinding surface will be discolored, due to food stains, irregularities, wear, etc. Only the center "black mark" will be gone. This central mark of the teeth is darkly colored enamel and not, as the old time horsemen believed, caused by decayed food. Foal's teeth have the black mark from the time they cut the gums.

A mature horse has forty teeth, twenty up and twenty down, twelve incisors, four tushes or canine teeth, and twenty-four grinders. The front teeth are known collectively as incisors or "nippers," because of the nipping action used when gathering grass. The horse siezes the grass in his front teeth and with a small, quick jerk of his head he "nips" off the grass. The nippers are placed in the front of both jaws. Six above and six below. They abut each other on the striking or grinding surface and do not overlap as do human teeth. The middle pair are called central incisors, the second pair are dividers, and the third pair are called corner nippers. The tushes or canine teeth, are arranged two on each side of the mouth, one in the upper jaw and one in the lower, after a short space of gum between them and the incisors. The space of gum for the bit, or the bars of the mouth, come next. Behind the bars, the grinders or molars begin.

The tushes have no use in the modern horse and often drop out after they have cut the gums. However, it is thought that these appendages may have once been used for self-defense and protection. Particularly since they are often lacking in mares and may be large in stallions. In the wild, the stallions are the herd protectors. When the tushes are present in mares they are usually quite rudimentary, especially in the upper jaw.

When a foal is born he will usually have no teeth, though a few foals may be born with a nipper or two, particularly if he is overdue. Assuming that the foal is born without any teeth, the first two teeth will appear in about eight days. These are the central nippers. At about six weeks the divider nippers will appear.

New teeth are very sharp at the outer edge and slant slightly in toward the mouth, making a sloping edge from front to back. The new teeth are rounded toward the outside and slightly hollowed toward the mouth.

At two months of age, the center nippers will be fully up and the dividers will shortly catch up to them. The corner nippers appear between the sixth and eighth months.

At the end of six months, the center and divider nippers are beginning to wear level. The black mark is also beginning to change its shape. Originally, the mark is long and narrow, but at about six months, it becomes shorter, wider, and much fainter.

As for grinders, foals are sometimes born with two grinders in each jaw, or they appear within two or three days after birth. After one month, another grinder appears in each jaw and after one year, a fourth.

At eighteen months, the central nipper mark is short, wide and faint and all the nippers are worn flat. At about two years, the colt will shed the two central nippers and his second set or permanent teeth will appear, and the fifth grinders will come in. At three year, the dividers will shed and the last grinder appears. At four years, the corner nippers drop. The tushes also appear about four years of age. At five yeas old, the teeth are fully up, and it is often said that the horse has a perfect mouth. At about six years, the mark in the central nippers disappears, the teeth being worn down into the outer enamel. At seven years, the mark is worn from the dividers, and at eight years, the mark is gone from the corners.

Age is primarily determined by the nippers, as the grinders are too difficult to see.

The upper nippers wear a bit slower than do the lower, primarily because only the lower jaw moves during chewing and the friction on the uppers is not as great. After eight years of age, the more experienced horsemen can somewhat determine age by the upper nippers. At nine years, the middle nippers have only a faint central mark, but the corners have one that is more easily seen. The corner teeth on the upper nippers also begins to show a surface curve. At ten, the middle mark of the central nippers has become nearly round, and at eleven, the mark of the corners is likewise.

To review: At the end of the first year, the foal has cut twelve nippers, and sixteen grinders, four in each jaw. At the beginning of the third year, the first grinders are shed and replaced and the fifth one appears. At the end of the third year, the sixth grinder also appears. At five years, the third grinders are shed and replaced. The fifth and sixth grinders are permanent and are not shed.

Usually only very experienced horsemen can discern age after nine years, and between the ages of nine and fifteen years it is very difficult. However, at the age of fifteen it again becomes easier for those familiar with horses to determine their age. At fifteen, all of the nippers have changed shape, and instead of being oval, they have become triangular, the pointed edge of the triangle being inward and the broadest side outward.

As the age of a horse progresses, the position of the teeth also changes. The teeth begin to elongate and jut forward as they begin to become triangular. Often they no longer strike evenly, the uppers sometimes overlapping the lowers and causing a "pig jaw" effect. This can often cause an untrue strike of the grinders, and causes chewing difficulty. This is one reason for having a yearly floating or trimming of the teeth.

Another mark whereby to tell a horse's age is Galvayne's groove or Galvayne's mark. This is a brown stained groove that appears at about eight years of age, at the gum line of the corner nippers. The groove travels down the length of the tooth until the age of twenty, when it again disappears.

There are several ways of altering a horse's mouth to make him appear younger than he is, but the most common method is called *bishoping*, after the man who invented this particular method. The teeth will have an artificial groove dug into them with an engraver's tool and then the groove will be burned with a heated iron until the required blackness is acquired. Though the horse does not feel much of this operation, the mark is, nevertheless, very deceptive to all but the practiced eye. To anyone else, the horse will appear to be a much younger animal than he really is.

One way to spot a bishoped horse is to check the shape of the teeth. The roundness and sharp edges of a younger horse's teeth cannot be reproduced in an older horse's teeth, as can the bishoped mark.

Though this is not done to much extent any more, changing the marks of horse's teeth was quite a common thing less than a hundred years ago. When the horse was the only mode of transportation, one often tried to get top dollar for any animal he happened to have for sale, and marking or bishoping a horse to get top dollar was often the only way.

There are few diseases that will trouble a horse's teeth, and cavities or dental caries are seldom seen. However, once in a while, one will find a horse with an abcessed tooth. This usually presents itself in the form of a puff on the outside of the face on the jaw containing the offending tooth. However, the puff need not always be present. A horse that has a constant draining from the nose, with no cold being present, should also be suspected. Should you have a horse that quids a lot, that is, chewing his hay then spitting it out without swallowing it, you might check for abcesses of his teeth. Quidding is a good sign of abcess.

Faulty construction of the mouth may also produce a condition that makes feeding difficult. The condition is called *parrot mouth*, and the horse is born with it. Do not confuse it with the "pig jaw" condition of advanced age. Parrot mouth is a condition where the upper teeth of the horse do not properly abut the lower ones. Instead, the upper teeth jut out and form an overbite. This often causes the lower teeth to strike the gums behind the upper teeth, instead of making contact with them, and this constant bumping against the gums by the lower teeth may bring on a condition called *lampas*. Lampas is a large, spongy swelling of the gums just behind the front teeth. The lump is caused by an influx of lymph and blood to the irritated part of the roof of the mouth. Naturally, the more often the striking of the teeth occurs against the lump, the larger the lump is going to get. Lancing by a veterinarian is the usual cure for lampas and feeding a laxative diet for a few days afterward is advisable. However, the horse with a parrot mouth seems prone to recurrences of lampas. Parrot mouth is called that because the overhang of the teeth resembles the structure of a parrot's beak.

As far as the bars of the mouth are concerned, there is little to be said about them, except that they should be checked after each ride to see that they have not been rubbed open by the action of the bit. Also, it is perfectly safe to insert the fingers in the space between the incisors and grinders to open the horse's mouth for examination or bitting. The best way to make a horse open his mouth for examination is to insert the fingers and place them flat on the top of the tongue, then slide the thumb under the tongue and turn the tongue up so that it touches the roof of the horse's mouth. He should open and stand quietly, with little resistance. It is a simple trick. Not many horses are about to pull on their own tongue to try and get away. Another way, this one usually used for bitting purposes, it to place the fingers on top of the tongue and press down. The horse should open for the bit. You may get the horse to the point that just a touch on the side of the tongue with one finger will cause him to open his mouth for the bit.

In any event, the mouth of the horse needs yearly care and attention, and you should include professional checkups in your regimen of horse care.

"The Age in Verse"

Two middle "nippers" you behold
Before the colt is two weeks old;
Before eight weeks two more will come;
Eight months, the "corners" cut the gums.

The outside grooves will disappear
From middle two in just a year;
In two years, from the second pair;
In three, the corners, too, are bare.

At two, the middle "nippers" drop;
At three, the second pair can't stop;
When four years old the third pair grows;
At five, a full new set he shows.

The deep black spots will pass from view,
At six years, from the middle two;
The second pair at seven years;
At eight, the spot each "corner" clears.

From middle "nippers" upper jaw,
At nine the black spots will withdraw;
The second pair at ten are white;
Eleven finds the "corners" light.

As time goes on the horsemen know
The oval teeth tree-sided grow;
They longer get, project before
Till twenty, when we know no more.

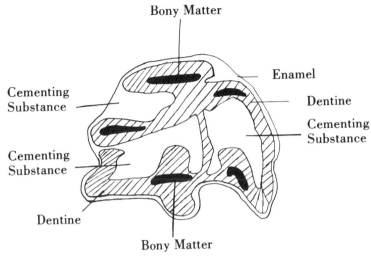

Crosscut of grinder or molar.

Foal's mouth – 1 to 2 weeks of age.

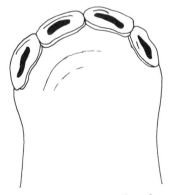

Foal's mouth – 6 weeks of age.

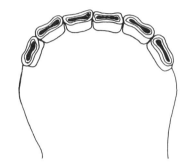

Foal's mouth – 8 months of age.

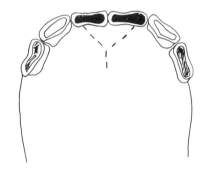

First permanent teeth – 2 years of age.

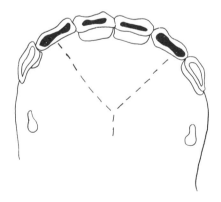

Second permanent teeth – 3 years of age.

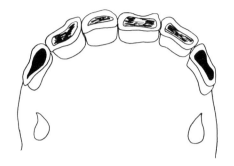

All permanent teeth − 5 years of age.

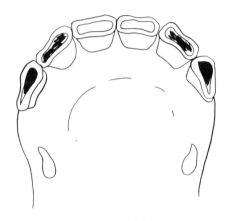

6 years old.

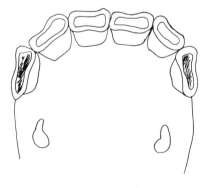

7 years old.

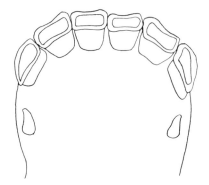

8 years old.

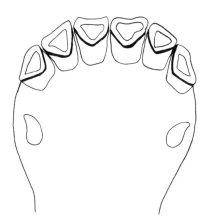

12–16 years old.

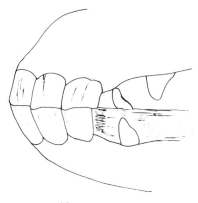

About 6 years old.

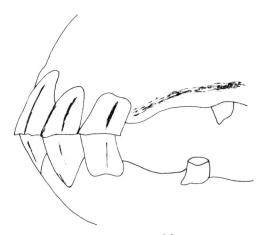

8 years old.

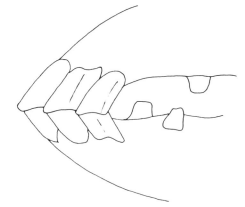

12 years old.

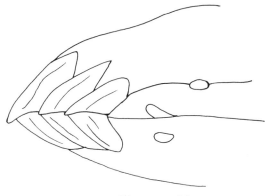

20 years old.

9
TACK

The equipment used in riding or driving a horse such as saddle, saddle pad, bridle, bit, headstalls, reins, or harness, are all considered to be the horse's tack. The word tack is really a corruption of the English word *tackle*, meaning equipment or gear, and next to the care and well-being of the horse, should come the care and maintenance of his tack. Regardless of how much or how little you may have spent in purchasing your equipment, the most important thing is the upkeep of the equipment after it has been purchased. Even relatively inexpensive equipment deserves to be well cared for, and will give you much better wear and service if you do so. One of the first things to consider when thinking about the care of tack is how to properly store it. Saddles, bridles, etc. should never be heaped in the corner, nor should they be left in aisles, alleyways, or in empty stalls. Saddles should not be tossed down in the nearest convenient spot after a ride, to await cleaning either. Each saddle and bridle should have its own rack and hook, and all brushes and grooming equipment should be kept in a neat, orderly container or bin, and not tossed down among the other equipment. Even if your saddle is dirty and you cannot clean it immediately after a ride, it should be placed on its proper rack to await cleaning. This applies to bridles, pads, blankets, etc.

Depending upon your particular stable set up, the saddles and bridles may be placed wherever it is easiest to get at them. However, the best method for storage is to have a tack room. There you should keep all necessary items of tack and grooming supplies, as well as your stable medicine chest. Saddle racks and hooks may either be purchased at tack shops or saddleries, or you

164

Excellent method for storage of saddles in a tack room.

can make them yourself. Many can be made quite simply and for less money than you would spend to buy one already made. The ones that you would purchase can be either the metal wall rack type, or the free-standing, wooden floor models. Some floor models are also made of metal and may be on large wheels or casters for ease of movement. These, however, are rather expensive and I have found that it is more economical to make your own. Wall racks can be made, quite simply, from two pieces of one inch water pipe joined at a right angle by an elbow, and fastened to the wall with large industrial brads or staples. This type of rack holds the saddle when in use and swings flat against the wall, out of the way, when not in use. These are good racks to have when you have a limited amount of space to use for a tack room. This type can be hung above things, such as tack, and medicine chests, and trunks, and still be out of the way. The free-standing variety of saddle rack may be made out of a regular wooden sawhorse that has been well padded, possibly with an old blanket wrapped around, and tied at both ends with baling twine. Another good method is to purchase a free-standing metal towel rack, put it together, and use it for a saddle rack. Most of these towel racks even have a small shelf underneath that is handy for storing smaller items like hunt hat, a pair of spurs, a tin of saddle soap, or a can of chrome or brass cleaner.

Bridle racks may also be purchased, as may bridle hooks, or again, you can economize and make your own quite easily and simply. One of the simplest of bridle racks is made by driving two twenty penny nails into the area where you want to hang your bridle, placing them two inches apart and one-half of their length into the wall. Then you simply hang your bridle upon them. A semicircle of wood may also be nailed to the wall and the bridle hung from it. The piece of wood should be about an inch thick so that the bridle does not slip off and about four inches across at the base. It should also be well-seasoned so that no resin escapes and seeps onto the bridle.

Wooden saddle racks that are stationary on the wall, can also be made by nailing, screwing or gluing together two pieces of wood that have had the edges mitered, so that together, they form a house roof effect. The pitch of the mitering should be such that the saddle rests on the saddle rack in the same position as it does on the horse. That is, with the padding of the underside supporting the weight of the saddle and not the gullet.

As for the actual care of the saddle and other equipment, all equipment should be kept clean and well oiled. The first thing that you should do after purchasing a piece of equipment is to oil it well with neatsfoot oil. This will begin the softening process that is so necessary to the proper breaking in of new tack. Tack used without first a good oiling is much more liable to crack or break under the strain of usage than would leather that has first been properly conditioned. Leather that is curved or bent in one position, such as the tabs on cheekpieces that attach the bit to the headstall, is especially prone to drying and cracking because of the bent position. Of course, tack should be cleaned thoroughly after each ride and never be put away dirty or wet. Saddles and bridles should be stripped down and given a thorough saddle soaping and polishing after each use, and the chrome or brass stirrup irons and bit shanks should be polished with either chrome cleaner or brass polish. Bridles should be taken apart at least once a week, the bit removed and thoroughly washed, and all joints, except those placed into the horse's mouth, should be oiled, then dried with a cloth. The headstall itself should be given a complete inspection with each weekly dismantling to see that no weak or cracked spots have developed. The bridle may be cleaned in tact after each ride if you do not have the time to totally dismantle it more than once a week, but be sure to clean well around the bit and the reins where they attach to the bit, as these are most often the first places in the headstall to show wear and dryness. Also, do not forget to soap and polish your girth, if it is leather, or brush it well and launder it once a week, if it is web or duck. A clean girth is a must if you are to keep your horse from becoming galled by the deposits of salt, sweat and dirt that build up on his girth when not taken care of properly. Be sure to soap well around the stitching of saddle, bridle, and girth, taking care to see that dirt and sweat has not accumulated and dried around buckles and dees. Buckles that are hard to bend, and/or buckle, or dees that will not swivel properly, show that the tack has been neglected or improperly cleaned. Saddle pads, too, should be cleaned thoroughly after each ride. If the pad is wet when the ride is over, allow it to dry, either on a drying rack, or on its own rack in the tack room. When it is dry, brush it well with a stiff brush (not one of the horse's), and clean away any dirt, scurf, or dried sweat that has accumulated there. Some pads may be washed (read tag or label when you buy one), and that should be done once a month. For those that are not washable, a good brushing will keep the pad in use for a longer time than were it not brushed or cared for.

Leg bandages and tail wraps should be washed after each usage and after they dry, should be rerolled so that they are ready for instant use. There is nothing more embarrassing than being asked to take your horse somewhere at the last minute and finding that you only have dirty bandages with which to wrap his legs and/or tail. Washing properly (by hand or on warm-cold cycle in the machine) also helps the bandage retain its stretchiness and flexibility. Rugs or blankets, too, should be brushed and dried well after each use, and should never be put away wet or damp, as they are certain to mold or mildew, as will any equipment that is allowed to remain damp or is stored in a damp place. Blankets should be aired regularly over a line, preferably in the sun, then brushed well before restoring. The brushing removes any mold or mildew spores that may have begun to grow on the blanket, or, if the blanket or rug is in nearly constant use, it cleans and fluffs both the lining and the outer blanket as well. Sheets and unlined blankets should be washed frequently for the same reason.

Tack styles and design depend on how you ride — English or Western, for pleasure or show — and even here the catagories are broken down further. If you ride English, do you ride to hunt, just to hack, or perhaps you ride saddle seat? If you ride Western, do you rope, barrel race, or just pleasure ride? Each style or type of riding has its own modification in its tack, though the Western saddles do not vary to as great a degree as do the English ones.

Saddles: The English *flat* or *park* saddle is one of the best types of saddles to learn to ride on, as this type of saddle gives you the closest contact with the horse. The park saddle has no knee rolls and little padding beneath the flaps to interfere with the contact between the rider's legs and the horse's body. Sercurity in this type of saddle can only be gained by learning the proper dependency on your own legs, feet, and balance, rather than upon the support of the saddle. The seat of the flat saddle is fairly shallow, the flaps nearly straight without any forward curve, and has little padding under the flaps between horse and rider.

The *forward seat* saddle is designed for the person who wants to hunt, jump, or show jump. The seat is deeper than that of the flat saddle and the flaps are curved forward toward the front of the horse. This saddle is equipped with knee rolls or thick rolls of leather that give support to the legs, and help to keep the rider from sliding forward on the horse's neck while jumping. While the forward seat saddle gives the rider more support than does the flat saddle, many people who learn on one never learn to depend upon themselves for balance and grip. Rather, they depend upon the knee rolls and padding to keep them aboard the horse. A prop is no substitute for learning to ride properly. Only after you have learned to ride and to depend upon yourself, do I suggest that you go on to a forward seat saddle. You will be a better rider in the long run if you learn properly first.

The *saddle seat* or *cut back show* saddle is used on gaited and equitation horses, and appears much like the park or flat saddle, except that the throat of the saddle is cut back to allow for total play of the horse's withers. From the top, the throat of the saddle appears to be cut away in a *U* shape. The flaps are straight and a bit longer than those of the flat saddle, and the rider sits further back on the horse's back when riding, nearly being over the animal's loins.

The *Western stock* saddle has a deep seat, a fairly high cantle, a wide pommel, or knee roll if you will, and a horn. The flaps are long and of a fairly even width down to the stirrups. Many Western saddles have a double cinch that fastens in two places on the horse's body. The first cinch fastens in the normal position, just behind the forelegs, but the second cinch, or girth, fastens around the horse's belly and should only be tight enough to touch the horse's stomach when the saddle is empty. It should never be tight enough to bind or cut the belly, or so that you cannot get two fingers between it and the horse with some semblance of ease. A *single cinch* Western saddle is often referred to as a *single-fire* rig, while the one with two girths is often called a *double-fire* rig. One with the cinch set back further than normal may be referred to as a *center-fire* rig. Many Western saddles are very ornately tooled, and the variety of patterns in the tooling are endless. Some Western saddles will have cantles that are lower than other and may be more swept back, and these are mainly used by people who use their horses for working on ranches, or in exhibitions such as for calf-roping, etc. The low cantle makes it easier to dismount quickly during timed events.

Bridles— Bridles differ even more greatly than do saddles, in both design and usage.

The *English snaffle* or *hunting snaffle* is a center jointed bit with large, round bit rings. This is one of the easiest bits on the horse's mouth when used properly. The action is on the corners of the horse's mouth and the large bit rings keep the bit from sliding into or through the horse's mouth should he open his mouth while bridled.

The D ring or *egg-butt snaffle* has bit rings shaped like a letter *D*. The purpose of this design is to keep the bit rings from pinching the sides or corners of the horse's mouth. The action is the same as the hunting snaffle.

The *full-cheek snaffle* has long bars that extend both upward and down from the bit rings, and these also keep the bit from pinching and produce a much sharper turn when galloping as the rounded ends of the bars press against the horse's cheek when he is turned. Full cheeks are seen quite a bit in timed jumping events where ground-saving turns are a necessity.

The *kimberwicke* is a bit that is used when the horse needs more control than a snaffle, yet less than a pelham. The action of the kimberwicke is on the bars of the horse's mouth and the bit has a low port for control. Most kimberwicke's have *D* rings so that they do not pinch, and all have a curb chain. Kimberwicke's, however, should not be used on a horse that has a tendency to pull, as they may make the horse lean on the bit, instead of responding or yielding to it. The best bit for a pulling horse is a pelham.

The *pelham* bit is used for a horse that requires more control than available with a snaffle. Most pelhams have a straight mouthpiece, though they are available in half-moon or port styles, and they have long shanks. Pelhams are used with double reins, though some more advanced riders may be seen using a device called a *converter* on their pelhams. Pelhams combine both the snaffle effect with the curb effect, the curb effect's severity is determined by how tightly the curb chain is fastened. The curb chain of a bit fits across the bars of the lower jaw, just behind the horse's chin. The looser the chain, the less the curb effect, the tighter the chain the more severe the curb. A converter for the pelham is a loop of leather with a buckle at each end. The rein is buckled around the center of the converter and the converter is attached to both rings of the bit. Thus, the bit can be used with one rein, yet achieve the same effect as with two. If the hands are raised, the converter acts upon the top bit ring and produces a snaffle effect on the horse's mouth. If the hands are lowered the bit action is on the bottom of the shank and produces a curb effect.

There are also variations of the pelham such as the Tom Thumb pelham, which has short shanks and is more severe, the Little Joe Weisenfeld pelham with a caveson curb effect, the curb chain being attached to the caveson, crisscrossing under the chin, and attaching to the bit rings from there.

Snaffles, too, differ in the thickness of the mouthpiece. The thicker the mouthpiece the easier on the horse, and the thickness may vary from the thickness of a man's thumb to the thinness of two pieces of ordinary fence wire. Some mouthpieces are straight, while others are twisted. Some snaffles are thin twists of wire and may even be double snaffles on one bit ring. These are best left strictly to the professional or not used at all.

Another type of English bit is the *bridoon* or *double bridle*. This is really the use of two bits at one time. A fairly thin snaffle and a straight mouth pelham are used on the same headstall at the same time. The double bridle is used to get the utmost response from the horse and increase sensitivity between horse and rider. Some hunters and jumpers are used with bridoons and nearly all equitation and gaited horses are ridden with them.

Some English bits have rubber mouthpieces, and English colt bits are all rubber over rawhide-cored mouthpieces. These are extremely flexible and will produce a very easy mouth. In fact, this author is well acquainted with a horse that is nine years old, and can be ridden anywhere in a colt bit.

Other parts of English tack are *martingales*. One type of martingale is the *standing martingale*. This is a single piece of leather attached to the girth on one end and to the horse's noseband on the other, and is held in place by a neck strap around the base of the horse's neck. Its main function is to keep the horse from raising its head too high and avoiding the bit. The *running martingale* is fastened to the horse in the same manner as the standing martingale, in that, it is fastened to the girth and held in place by a neck strap, but it is not connected to the horse's noseband. Rather, the strap from the girth to the noseband divides halfway up its length, and a ring is attached to both ends of the divided leather. The reins pass through these rings and the action produced by drawing back on the reins pulls the horse's nose down and back toward his chest.

The *Irish martingale* is a simple, small leather strap with a ring at each end. One rein passes through each ring and this martingale is just to keep the reins from being tossed to one side of the horse's neck, such as during jumping. The martingale usually fits just across the width of the horse's windpipe, not being attached to the horse in any way, except that it slides freely back and forth on the reins and keeps them in the proper position, one on either side of the horse's neck.

Western bridles vary even more than do the English bits and bridles. The standard Western bit and bridle is a simple headstall with a browband and throat latch and a low port, flat shank curb bit. From there, however, things can get a bit more fancy and complicated. Headstalls may come in a one-eared or two-eared variety, that is, having just one loop of leather around one ear or two, and no throat latch or noseband. Bridles that have nosebands may have thick ones, or very thin wire ones that are plastic-coated, they may be placed high or low on the face depending upon what they are being used for. The bits may be flat-shanked or round-shanked, they may have gradually curved bit shanks, or have hard recurves, and the mouthpieces may be low port, high port, a half-breed port with a cricket or roller in the mouthpiece. There may even be *spade bits* that have very high ports, most of them with rollers in them.

As you can see, there are many types of tack, but one thing applies to all tack, and that is its good care. The following photographs give you a step by step lesson in cleaning a saddle, and I hope they will prove to be useful to you.

The first thing to do is to remove the leathers from the safety bars. Next you should wet your sponge, rub it well over your cake of saddle soap and work up a good amount of lather. Beginning at the front of the saddle, begin applying soap in brisk, swirling strokes. Be sure to clean well around all areas of hard wear and stitching lines. The soap should be applied to all smooth leather parts of the saddle. The underside of stitched binding should not be overlooked in the cleaning process. Holding the saddle upside down in the lap to clean the gullet and padding provides a stable surface and affords a good grip. One of the most important places to be sure to keep clean is the throat of the saddle, as dirt has a tendency to collect there. Stitching that takes a lot of stress should be cleaned also, such as that keeping the padding in. Do not forget to thoroughly clean the rear of the gullet. Dirt collects there too. Billet straps take a lot of stress and strain, and must be kept clean and pliable. The underside of the skirts should not be neglected in the cleaning process.

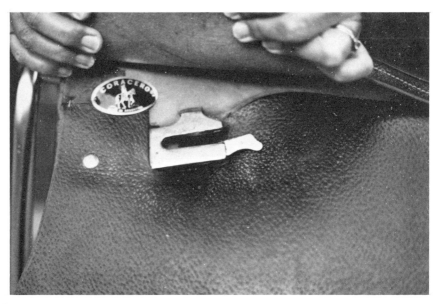

Leathers should be removed from saddles and safety bars opened when preparing to clean tack.

Work up a good lather on the cleaning sponge.

Soap the leather well.

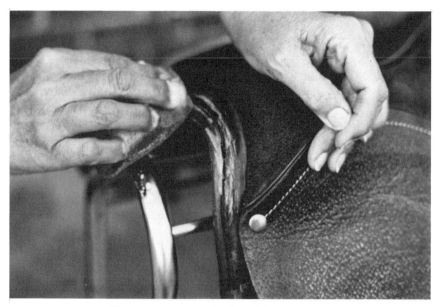

Clean well at stitched or folded parts

Skirts should be cleaned thoroughly to preserve suppleness.

The padding at the rear of the saddle should not be neglected in the cleaning of the saddle.

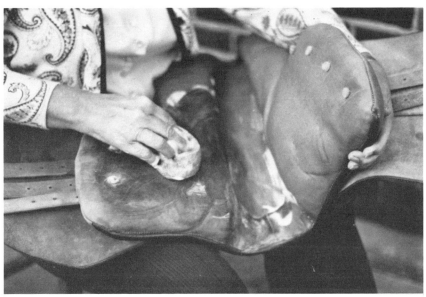

The underside of the saddle should receive very careful attention when being cleaned.

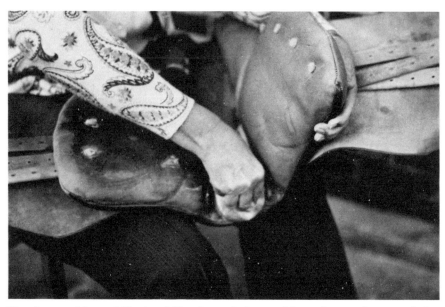

The throat of the saddle should be cleaned thoroughly as this is where much dirt and sweat collects.

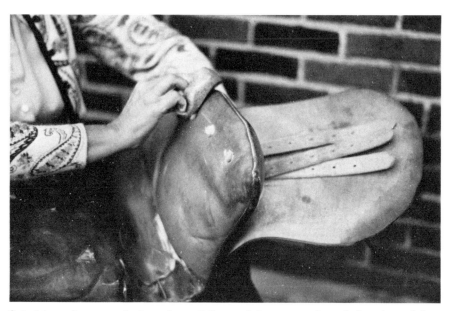

Stitching edges must be kept free of dirt and dryness and good cleaning of these areas aids greatly in increasing the life of the saddle.

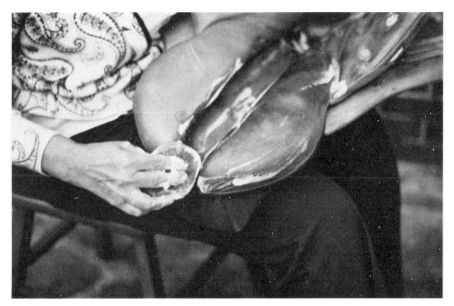

The tail of the saddle should not be forgotten in the process.

Billet straps, too, should be soaped thoroughly.

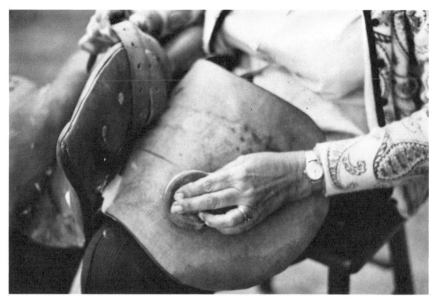

The underside of the skirts gets very dry; so be sure to clean them well.

The drying and buffing process is as important as the cleaning itself, as soap that is allowed to dry onto tack will soon form a dulling film or scum on your tack. Billets should be dried thoroughly so that all scum is removed. The gullet should be wiped out well, so that dust or any dirt in the horse's coat will not cling to it. Dirt will also cling to folded or tucked under sections of the saddle, such as at the rear of the gullet, so it is important to dry and buff well there too. A good rubbing will shine the top of the saddle.

Stirrup leathers, too, must be cleaned, and the only way to do that properly is to remove them from the saddle and remove the irons from them. A good lather here is also necessary to a good shine. Clean around the stitching well, also around the buckles themselves. Drying the buckles helps to prevent rust from forming around them, and buffing the stitching assures that no soap film will remain to collect dust or dirt.

The girth, also, needs careful cleaning, especially if it is heavily stitched and/or folded leather. Here, too, the stitching around the buckles is especially important, as they take a lot of strain and must be kept in good condition. Buckles on elastic-ended girths must not be neglected. Drying metal buckles is very important in reducing the chances of rust. Then the rest of the girth should be buffed off well. The stirrups should then be placed on the leathers, and the leather replaced on the saddle. Safety bars should be closed. The saddle is now clean and ready to be racked or used.

When drying and polishing the tack do not neglect any hidden or unseen places.

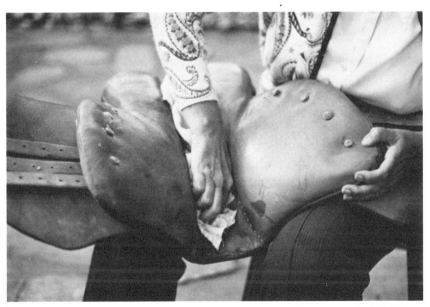

Remove any soapy residue from folded areas; as old soap will hold dirt.

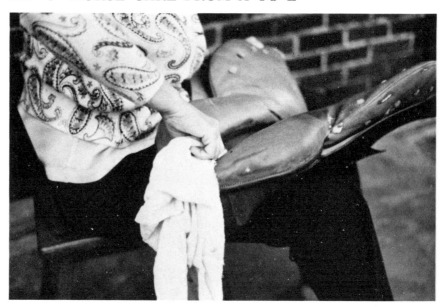

Dust and dirt tend to collect readily on soap scum if not removed from the tail of the saddle.

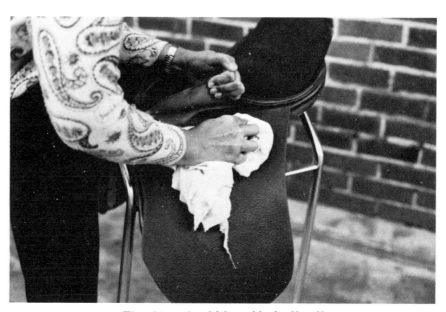

The skirts should be rubbed off well.

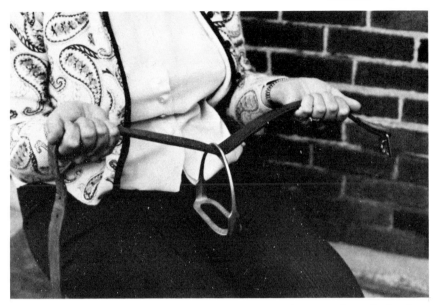

Stirrup leathers should now be attended to. Remove the irons from the leathers.

Soap the leathers well, including both narrow edges.

Again; soap well all stitched areas.

Buckles may be washed off as well and the fold of leather around the buckle needs particular attention.

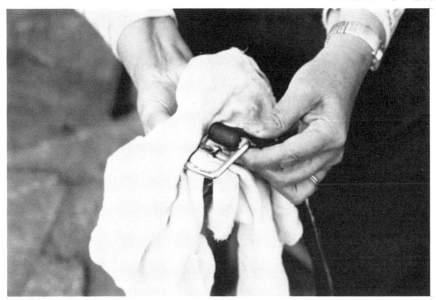

Be sure to dry the area around the buckle well so that it does not rust.

Do not allow soap scum to remain in stitching as it has a tendency to collect dirt and to dry the stitches.

The girth is next to be cleaned.

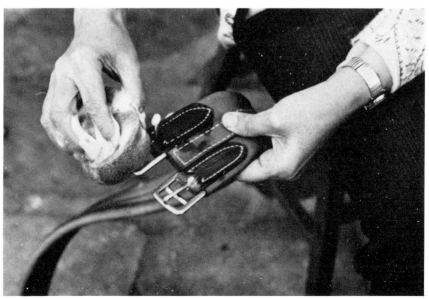

Here again; the buckles and stitching should be carefully taken care of.

Girths with elastic ends should have the leather tabbed buckles cleaned, but care should be taken not to get soap on the elastic as it will dry out.

Buckles may then be cleaned with chrome or brass cleaner.

The entire length of the girth should be dried and polished.

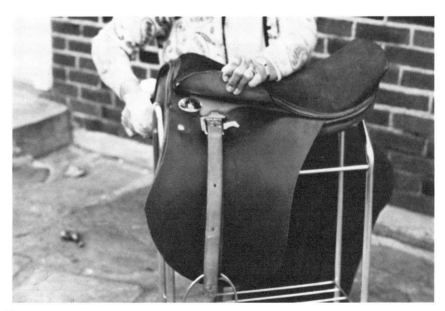

The iron may now be replaced on the leather and the leathers reattached to the saddle.

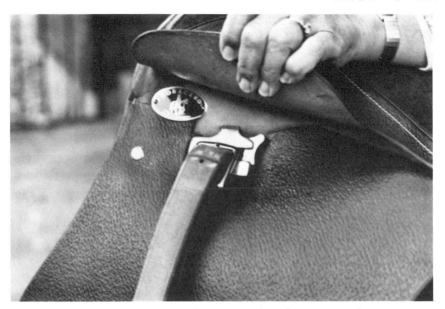

Safety bars should be closed again so that they are not forgotten.

The leathers should be run up and the saddle racked to await its next usage.

Another all-important aspect of tack is the fit. In order to be right for the horse, the tack must fit properly. Tack that is too small or too large, tack that pinches or slips, or tack that rubs, will all do damage to either you or your horse. Saddles should not be placed too far forward on the withers because they can bind against the neck. This restricts the movement of the shoulders and puts your weight too far forward on the withers of the animal, thus upsetting his center of gravity or balance. Too, saddles should not be placed way behind the withers so that the girth has to be drawn toward the hindquarters to be tightened. Saddles placed here, place the rider's weight over the kidneys, and cause undue strain on the horse. A properly fitted saddle will span the withers, and the girth will be drawn straight up for fastening with the forward edge of the girth about an inch and a half, to two inches from the horse's elbow. Bits and bridles, too, must fit correctly in order to do their job efficiently and still be comfortable on the horse. Bridles should fit so that the bit just barely wrinkles the corners of the horse's mouth, the throat latches should be no tighter than the span of three fingers between the latch and the horse's jaws, and browbands should permit the horse full use of his ears, both in forward and back position.

As you can see, tack is a very important part of a well cared for horse.

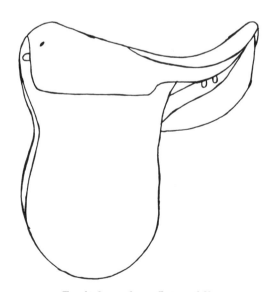

English park or flat saddle.

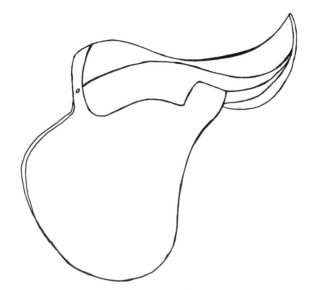

English forward seat.

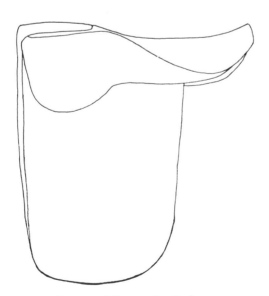

Show saddle—cut back throat.

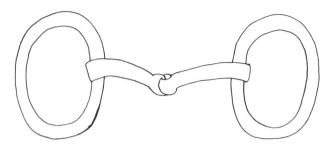

English hunting snaffle.

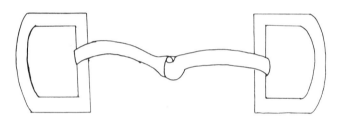

D ring or Egg-Butt snaffle.

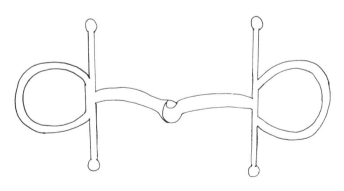

Full Cheek snaffle.

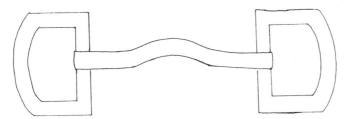

Kimberwicke bit.

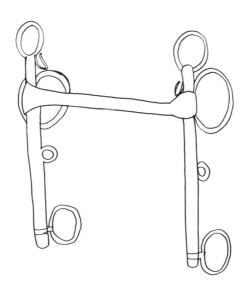

English pelham.

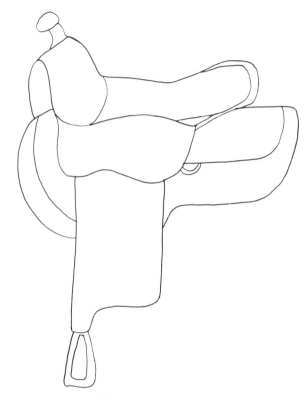

Western Stock saddle.

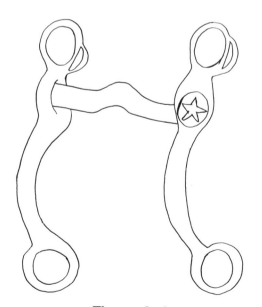

Western Curb.

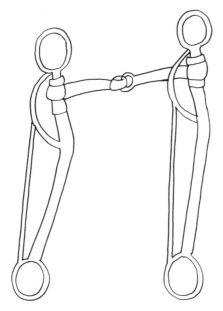

Western Loose Cheek snaffle.

10
THE STABLE: ROUTINE AND MAINTENANCE

As in all facets of horse care, the care of the stable and the routine should proceed on a regular, orderly basis, and on a well-kept schedule. The stable itself should be well built, airy, light, tidy, and in general, a pleasant place for the horse to spend his time, for unless out to pasture, the horse does spend most of his time in the stable. Stall should be roomy (ten feet by ten feet minimum and twelve feet by twelve feet preferred), and as safely constructed as possible.

If one has no stable, but wishes to build one, how should this be undertaken? Or, if one has a stable, but wishes to build or remodel the stalls, how is this to be done? First of all, in building a stable, the site that it is to stand upon is very important. Stables should not be built in areas that receive a lot of drainage from other areas, such as in gulleys, or ravines at the bottom of hills. Neither should they be built where they will take the full force of the weather such as rain, sleet, snow, and blazing summer heat. The ideal place to build a stable is where it is level and where the stable will be somewhat sheltered from the full effects of weather, yet, will receive good light and plenty of air, and remain dry. However, many of us are not blessed with property that has all of the perfect requirements. Most of us need to make do with whatever property we happen to own. However, you should know how to pick the best site on whatever property you have. First, look for the most level piece of ground that will have the best drainage. Good drainage is one of the most important aspects of stable maintenance. That is why if you are faced with only two choices, building at the top of a hill, or building at the bottom, you should build at the top. If you build at the bottom of the hill, not only will your stable drainage have nowhere to go, but you will get all of the water that drains down from the hill as well, and this may mean constantly wet or flooded stall floors in wet weather. One of the best solutions, if you do not have any really level land to build upon, is to build a *bank barn* or stable. This type of housing is usually bilevel, and the barn is partly built into, or under, the side of the hill. The lower level, where the stalls are, is cut into the side of the hill. This helps to provide shelter and warmth for the barn, and the bank barns are the easiest barns to keep warm in the cold months of winter. The upper level will be flush with the top of the hill, and will be one story on the hill, or back side, and two stories over the front, or drop off the side of the hill.

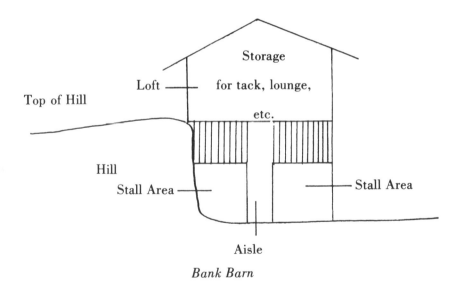

Bank Barn

If you have level land, there are many varieties of barns and stables to choose from. (See diagrams at end of chapter). As well, there are a variety of building materials, such as wood, stone, brick, cinder or cement block, and contoured metal. The type of material you choose will depend largely upon your particular location, and how much you wish to spend on building your stable.

To begin building a stable, you should first have a foundation dug, and the footing should be placed below the frost line so that the freezes and thaws of the ground do not heave the foundation and stable out of place or line. (Check with your county agent in your area for depth of frost line.) The footing or foundation should be of concrete or cement block. After the footing has been placed, the area where the stalls are to be located should be marked off, allowing for a wide center aisle if the stable is to have a double row of stalls, and the floor should be dug out with a backhoe to a depth of about eighteen inches. The dug out area should then be lined with flat rocks to a depth of about one foot. The rocks should be placed so that they form a flat, fairly close surface, then smaller rocks and stones should be placed in the pit to raise the level to about eight inches from the top. The small stones may be supplemented with some medium weight gravel if so desired or needed. The pit should now be brought to full level with dirt, and the dirt should be packed down so that it presents a flat, firm surface. The stalls may now be built on the prepared area. If you are using oak beams for the corners of the aisle stalls, you might wish to set them before the pit is completely filled in. This removes the necessity of having to dig up the floor again. If you are using metal posts for the corner, then concrete slabs should be prepared and seated into the corners of the stall before the pit is filled with the dirt, and the posts bolted or cemented onto them. This enables you to cover the cement slabs with dirt, and thus, create a flat floor over the entire stall area. This removes or prevents a tripping hazard, due to the corners of the cement slabs being covered with dirt rather than sticking out into the stall or barn aisle.

The stalls themselves should be constructed of two inch thick oak boards, about two feetwide, and placed one to two inches apart. Oak is the best material to build with, as it does not rot readily, and it is tough enough to withstand the abuse it will get from a horse. Even a playfully thrown kick can split regular board with little difficulty. Building with oak not only saves the constant replacing of broken boards, but also lessens the chance of the horse hurting himself by getting caught on a splintered board.

The boards should be placed from the floor to about withers height. This enables the horses to see what is going on, and yet,

An example of a safety hazard. The floor is badly worn and the square of concrete left from a removed corner post presents a bad tripping hazard.

Oak boards should be used to separate stalls. Oak is best because of its strength and resiliancy.

affords the best stall protection and confinement. From the top board to the ceiling, there should be placed rows of round, one inch metal bars set about three inches apart. This keeps the horses separated from each other, yet they can see, smell, and touch noses through the bars while staying out of trouble. Ceilings, by the way, should be about fourteen feet in height. This gives the horses head room, should they rear in the barn, yet, does not allow the body heat to escape too readily in the winter.

Doors on stalls that give directly to the outside may be of the half-door, or Dutch door variety. This is a type of door that may be opened at the top and remained closed at the bottom. This type of stall door is best for fretful horses who need to see out, or horses, due to some illness or injury, that cannot be allowed out. Doors on inside stalls should be of the rolling variety. These doors are constructed just like the stall, with bars from withers height to the top of the door, and they are hung on tracks. They are easily opened and shut by rolling them along the tracks, and they take up the least amount of space as they roll back along one side or the front of the stall.

Bars may be used to form stall tops. This allows the horse to see what is going on around him.

Half-doors, or Dutch doors as they are often called, are good for horses who need to be confined to the barn for a long period of time.

Stall doors on inside aisles may be hung on tracks by means of rollers which slide them back and forth for easy opening and closing.

A window in each stall is a must, but windows must all be guarded and should have the tilt variety of pane so thay they may be opened without having a draft blow directly on the horse. The window guards may either be metal bars or heavy wire mesh. Be sure, however, if you are using wire mesh that it is galvanized. Galvanizing welds all of the cross meshes to one another, and keeps the horse from getting his lips, tongue, etc. pinched in the metal if he rubs his face on the guards. The tilt variety of window, tilts out at the bottom and inward at the top when open, allowing air to circulate inward over the horse's heads. This provides good circulation of air in the barn, yet the air does not blow on the animals. Louvres, placed just under the eaves of the barn roof are also good for ventilation. Louvres that can be opened and closed at will are the best, for they may be opened on mild winter days to remove the stale air of the barn, and yet, keep out the wintry cold. In summer, they provide a constant air flow into and out of the barn, and keep the air from becoming stale and extremely hot and stuffy.

Lighting is another thing to think about when building a stable. Proper lighting is a must in any barn, both in the stalls and in the aisles. Proper lighting allows you to see clearly and recognize everything in the barn at first glance. The best type of lighting, other than natural daylight from windows and skylights, is florescent lighting for aisles, wash racks, crosstie and saddling areas, and for indoor arenas and training areas. Lights in stalls may be incandescent bulbs, but they should each have a wire shield that covers and protects the bulb. Skylights in the ceiling help supply light during the day. Florescent lights produce a much greater amount of light than do regular bulbs, and cost less to operate. Also, they burn cooler and cast less shadow than do regular bulbs.

Just as stall floors are important, so are the barn aisles. The aisles should be large or wide enought to easily turn a wheelbarrow around in, and in some larger barns, they may be wide enough to drive a truck through. The aisle floors themselves may be of many materials, such as dirt, concrete, or asphalt, with asphalt being preferred, as it can be kept clean like concrete, yet is not as slippery under metal shod hoofs. Dirt floors often wear away or develop ruts too quickly to be readily acceptable. Regardless of the construction of your aisle floor, there is one thing to take into consideration. Aisles must be kept clear and free of obstructions. Bales of hay, feed drums, etc. should not be stored in aisles or allowed to block them. Too, unused aisles that end as alleyways

Barn aisle should be wide and free from obstruction.

Aisles should never be blocked or cluttered like this.

Alleyways between stalls should never be used for storage of combustibles, such as hay or straw.

between stalls should not be used as a dumping place for moldy or unused hay, straw, or other stable material. One or two bales of bedding may be placed nearby when you are working in the stable and doing such chores as mucking out, or bedding down stalls, but they should not be allowed to remain there and should never block a stall doorway. While on the subject of stable maintenance, it is a good idea, also, to clean out regularly the cob webs and dust that will have a tendency to collect along the ceiling. It is not good to allow this to build up, for it is not only unsightly, but creates a health hazard for the horse should he inhale any of the matter contained in the webs.

Other good things to have in your stable are wash racks that double as grooming or saddling areas, or crosstie areas. Also, a foaling or isolation stall. A wash rack or crosstie area is very handy when you need to work on your horse outside the stall. Here you can crosstie him for bathing, clipping, saddling, shoeing, vet care, or any number of other reasons. The isolation stall is nearly indispensable if you need a place to house a new horse or one that is sick or injured. The stall should be at least one stall width away from the rest of your stalls, should be roomy, and should have a set

Stall doors should never be blocked or obstructed.

Webs that are allowed to collect like this hold dirt and are a health hazard.

of crosstie rings in the stall. Often an injured or sick horse will resist attention and will need to be restrained for treatment. The crossties in the stall are very handy. If you have no sick horses, but have mares that are in foal, then the oversized isolation stall can be used as a foaling stall. Most mares are glad of the extra room when giving birth.

Let us go back to the subject of windows for a moment. Windows should be placed so that the horse can see out. Horses that cannot see out soon become afraid of the outside and depend on their stalls to give them security. This is called stall courage or *agoraphobia*, meaning fear of the outside. Horses that can see outside, also tend to become less bored and less prone to nervous disorders caused by fretting.

Now, what about placement of feed and water equipment in the stall? Also, what type of equipment is best? First off, I do not recommend feeding hay from any position except the floor. Hay racks and mangers are hazards that the stable can well do without. The greater majority of hay racks are placed too high for safe feeding of hay, and mangers are too confining because of the dust found in hays.

Plastic or rubber feed tubs set in metal rings for stall corners or wall placment are the best method of feeding grain. The tub should be placed high enough so that the horse cannot get his feet into it, yet low enough so that he need not reach or strain to get at his feed. About chest height is right. The water bucket should be placed near, but not up against the feed tub. This enables the horse to eat and drink at his leisure without dribbling his grain all over his water. Hay should be fed nearest the door so that you can keep an eye on just how much is being eaten, and how long it takes him to consume his portion. By watching how much he eats and how long it takes him before he walks away, you can determine just how much hay to feed at each feeding and cut down on waste. If necessary, feed a bit less hay per feeding, but feed hay a bit more often, perhaps giving a bit in midmorning or midafternoon, rather than one lot at feeding time, and not having it consumed and go to waste. With a bit of practice, you will get to know just when, how much, and how often to hand out the hay, and you may find that your feeding bills are no greater with this method.

Water buckets may be secured to the wall, either by means of a large metal hook that has had the point sawed off, or by building a wooden shelf to hold it, and clipping the bucket to the wall by means of a rubber stall door guard. Buckets should be cleaned out regularly and scrubbed well with a stiff brush once a week. Each horse should have its own water bucket or automatic waterer, whichever is preferred, and should not have to share buckets or waterers. The reason for the nonsharing of water or feed buckets should be obvious. Colds, influenza, and other diseases are easily passed from one animal to another when water and feed buckets are shared or swapped. Always use the same bucket and/or feed tub for one specific horse, and do not swap or change around.

A good idea to keep a restless or fractious horse quiet and contented in the stall is to give him a toy to play with. While this may sound ridiculous, it is a good thing to remember. Stop and think for a moment. Suppose you were a horse and had a lot of idle time and were confined to a stall the better part of rainy, snowy days, or perhaps for some other reason. I am sure you would become awfully bored and restless with nothing to do but stand around and look out the window or at the horse in the next stall to yours. Toys for horses are easy and simple to make, safe, unbreakable, and easy to replace. One of the simplest toys to make is made from a plastic, half-gallon or gallon milk container. A few stones, about the size of an egg, or just small enough to fit down the neck or the jug, will do. Place the stones inside the jug and screw the cap on tight. Tie a piece of baling twine through the jug handle and hang the jug from the side of the stall at just above chest height. Many horses apparently enjoy butting the jug around to hear the rattle of the stones, and they can while away quite a bit of stall time with this type of toy. As with anything new, however, introduce the toy slowly and carefully. Show the empty jug to the horse and allow him to smell it before you insert the stones. Let him watch you place the stones in the jug and complete the operation of capping the jug and tying it in the stall. If he is allowed to watch what you are doing, the first rattle of the stones will come as less of a surprise when you shake the jug for him to hear the first time. He may be startled the first few times when he brushes against the jug hanging in the stall, but he will soon find that he can make the sound himself by bumping the jug with his nose, and it will not take him long to begin to play with his toy.

Another good toy is a soccer ball. Many horses enjoy playing with an old soccer ball in their stalls. Too, the ball is soft enough so that should the horse get bumped with it while playing, or should he lie down on the ball, he is not going to be hurt in the process. Toys, and balls in particular, should never be small enough so that the horse can pick them up in his mouth and perhaps swallow them and get them lodged either in his throat or intestines. Things such as tennis balls, golf balls, ping-pong balls, etc. should **never** be given to a horse as a toy. Any laced balls, such as footballs, should also not be given as a horse has a great deal of strength in his teeth, and should he bite through the lacing he may swallow some of them, or a part of the ball itself. Balls should also not be highly inflated. A bit underinflated is a good idea. Underinflate just enough to take the hardness out of the ball, yet leave in some of the bounce.

All facets of stable management and stable routine are important, and it is difficult to determine which ones are more important than others. One very important part of stable maintenance, however, is the construction of the stable, the stall size, and the stable equipment itself. One important thing to consider, other than the stall size, which is best at twelve feet by twelve feet, is the type of floor that the stall will have. The best type of floor is the dirt over stone-lined pit that was discussed earlier in the chapter. This type floor affords the best drainage possible. Plain dirt floors are also acceptable, even though they do not drain quite as efficiently as the dirt, overlined, pit type of floor. Many older barns, particularly those with standing stalls or tie stalls, and that were built around the turn of the century, had either wooden or hard floors such as concrete or brick. The bedding in these types of stalls is usually laid very thickly to prevent the horse from coming in contact with the hard floor underneath. Most of these stalls have a gutter running along the rear of the stall, and this takes the place of the dirt floor in draining of the stall. Too, these old type stalls sloped slightly downward at the rear to cause all of the stall wetness to gather in the drain. If the stables are kept immaculate and the bedding changed daily and the horse exercised vigorously each day, it cannot be said that these types of stables do damage to the horse. However, the ideal arrangement is to have a box stall for each horse so that he may, at will, lie down, get up, and walk around by himself. Stables that consist of rows of tie stalls or standing stalls are seldom seen today, and happily so, for most people do not have the time to properly care for a stable of standing stalls, or they cannot hire anyone to do the job for them. Caring for a standing stall stable requires much more precise cleaning and mucking out of the stalls than does the care of a stable of box stalls. Tie stalls should really be cleaned out to the bottom each day, as the manure and other waste has no room to be spread around the stall as in a box, and the bedding cannot be easily used over again as it is usually wet by the time it is cleaned out. Concrete floors are not good for stall use in most instances, as they do not afford any drainage unless the stall floor is tilted to the rear, and because they are very cold and of course hard. Standing on concrete over a long period of time is hard on the horse's legs and feet. Wooden floors are also not suitable to use for stalls, as they tend to hold moisture and stable odors and eventually they will rot away, causing a dangerous situation in weakness of the floor.

As mentioned before, I think that it is best to feed hay directly from the stall floor, rather than to feed hay from a hay rack or manger. Hay racks, while they do contain the hay well and they do keep the horse from eating his hay too quickly, also tend to force the horse to pull or yank his hay from them, and in doing so, he may be doing himself harm. Even the cleanest hay has bits and pieces of loose grasses and dustlike particles that have a tendency to drift into the animal's eyes and nostrils as he pulls the hay free from the pat in the rack. These bits and pieces can lodge in the eye and scratch it, and can be inhaled into the lungs where they can cause immeasurable trouble. Eating with the head pointed up-

Standard corner variety of hay rack.

Stable tools should be hung up out of the way when not in use.

ward is also not a natural position for the horse to feed from. In nature, the horse grazes and feeds with his nose downward.

Mangers, too, can cause trouble. Most mangers are made of wood, many of them solid and tightly constructed. Shaking out a pat of hay in such a confined spaced is bad for the horse, as he is certain to have to inhale some of the dust and hay bits while trying to take a mouthful of hay. Too, most horses chew their hay right where it was pulled from the pat, and in doing so, will be eating with his head in the manger and inhaling the dust before it settles back onto the rest of the hay. Too, horses that lie down in their stalls to rest, often roll over and get cast or stuck under their mangers and cannot get up again. This in itself should be reason enough to tear out the manger and feed hay from the floor. If, however, you want or need to use a manger for feeding hay, see to it that the sides of the manger are slatted and not of a solid piece of wood. This allows some of the dust to dissipate as the hay pat is pulled apart, and cuts down on the amount inhaled by the horse.

Others things also need to be considered when you think about stable maintenance. For example, tools. Every stable should have at least one wheelbarrow, a hose, a broom, several shovels, several rakes, and most important of all, a fire extinguisher or two.

Feed tub and manger set up.

Fire extinguishers should be placed in a prominent location at the end or middle of each stable aisle, and there should be one in the feed room or feed building, and one in the tack room. No stable should be without them. *No Smoking* signs, too, should be prominently displayed and their message strictly enforced. Smoking should not be allowed within less than fifty feet of the barn or storage buildings, and should never be allowed in the barn or lounge. Another necessity in any stable is the medicine chest. This should be kept either in the tack room or at one end of the barn or barn aisle. Emergency in the stable is not to be taken lightly and one should always be as well prepared for them as possible.

While fire is not pleasant at any time, it is an even greater hazard when it occurs in the stable. That is why it is a good idea to have a separate building for the storage of feeds, beddings, and other combustibles, rather than keeping them in the same building as the horses are housed in. A weeks ration of feed should be the absolute limit kept in the barn, and feeds and beddings should never be stored overhead in lofts. Hay fires burn very hot and very fast, and once started, are nearly impossible to contain or stop. Even when no smoking is strictly enforced and every safety precaution against fire is taken, there is always the chance of spontaneous combustion of the hay or bedding. This occurs when the hay has been slightly damp and cannot dry out, due to it being stacked together in a loft or building. The hay or straw begins to decay, which produces heat. The more it deteriorates, the more heat is generated, and before long, it will begin to burn of its own accord. It does not take long for spontaneous combustion to take place. A week may be sufficient if conditions are right and all too often the process goes unnoticed until it is too late. It is better to be safe than sorry, and to store feeds, grains, and bedding elsewhere.

Another aspect of stable routine and maintenance is the control of pests, and these include rodents as well as insects. Rats and mice can deplete feed supplies at a rapid rate, as well as carrying diseases that can be transmitted to both horse and man. Too, rodents like to chew leather, and valuable equipment can easily be lost to their gnawing teeth. If you have a great population of rodents, the best and simplest answer to the problem is to have a professional exterminator rid you of your problem. However, if your rodent trouble is not too bad, you can do it yourself by purchasing one of the many types of rodent poisons available on the market. Be sure, however, to keep all rodent control methods out of the reach of the horses and other livestock. Another good answer to the rodent problem is to keep a cat or two in the stable. Not only will they help keep down the rodent population, but they will also be extra company for your horse, particularly if yours is a one or two horse stable.

Flying insects are a real annoyance, perhaps even more so than the rodents, as they attack the horse directly. One of the best methods of keeping down the insect problem is to keep a clean stable. The less dirt and stable waste that is left lying around the better, for it is the stable waste that attracts the insects. Feeds should always be well covered, too, as sweet smelling feeds will attract flies and other pests. Stable wastes should be cleaned up as often as possible and disposed of properly, and the manure pile should not be placed too close to the barn or you will be defeating your purpose of keeping the barn clean. Uneaten feeds should not be allowed to stand around in tubs or buckets to go sour, for they, too, will attract pests. Any feeds, hays, or beddings that are moldy or unfit for use should either be burned or taken to the manure pile. Floors should be swept daily and the sweepings should also be disposed of on the manure pile, or in a sealed or lidded container. Daily fogging or misting of the barn with insect spray is a great help, especially in hot weather. Just be sure that all of the horses are removed from the barn before fogging, and that all feeds, hay, and water is removed or tightly covered. Sugarlike preparations are also available to assist in keeping down the insect problem and this, too, must be kept out of the reach of the horse. Daily application of an insect preparation directly to the horse's body is a must in hot weather, particularly before turning him out to pasture or before going for a ride. Special preparations made for horses should be used on the animals, as they are designed to work with the animal's body chemistry and not cause allergic reactions while doing the most effective job of insect control.

As mentioned before, it is a good idea to have water piped directly into the barn. Not just for ease of daily watering of the horse, but for convenience sake as well. It is much easier to treat

Water piped into the barn makes stable work much easier.

Old bathtubs make good watering troughs for paddocks, if they are cleaned daily.

Spring-fed watering troughs are ideal as the water is constantly flowing freely through them and is always fresh.

strains and sprains that need cold water applications if the water is right at hand. A good source of water should also be handy when the horse is confined to the paddock or corral. Here, too, he should be able to find water whenever he wants it, and old bath tubs make excellent watering troughs. They are easy to fill, easy to empty, and easy to keep clean. Another method of outside watering is a spring-fed watering trough. The water flows into and out of these in a steady flow, and the water never has a chance to get stagnant or old.

When not spending his time in the stable, the horse spends a good deal of time, or should spend a good deal of time, in pasture. One of the best grasses and one of the most widely used types of grass for pasture is rye grass. Rye grass is tough, hardy, quick growing, and well sustaining. Too, it is rich in vitamins and minerals and can survive long periods of drought without withering away. Most permanent pastures are planted with a rye grass mixture. Most contain several varieties of rye grass, some for hardiness, some for richness, and some for longevity, and these are mixed with other grasses, such as Kentucky bluegrass and specialized timothy. Of course, each section of the country will have its own particular blend of pasture seeding mixes, but rye is the most widely used as a basis for pasture. While Kentucky bluegrass is famous as a pasture, there are many sections of the country where it does not do well, due to the fact that it cannot withstand extreme heat without an equivalent amount of rainfall to replenish it. It does well where there is higher humidity.

Regardless of the type of pasture that your horse is on, it is important to know just how much pasture to allow, and when to start him on pasture. Spring grasses are rich in nutrients, but due to their rapid growth rate in spring, they are also highly laxative. Many horses that are put to pasture in early spring develop serious cases of scoured bowels, or severe diarrhea. Horses that are to be put out to spring grass need to be watched very carefully. A short time on pasture each day (fifteen to twenty minutes), for a week will suffice for starters. The horse's stools should be carefully checked and if they become very runny or quite green in color, it is best to stop the pasture for a week or two, or cut down the time on pasture until the grass begins to slow its growth rate and the horse's stools have returned to normal. After the first week, if the horse has not developed diarrhea, you may begin to increase the time that he is on pasture. Increase it gradually and keep an eye on his stools. As long as he remains normal and well on the pasture, you are doing the right thing. However, should he show signs of scours or diarrhea, cut down his time until he stabilizes. The first rush of growth is over in a few short weeks, and once the pasture has slowed, then the horse may be turned out for the length of time he is to be allowed daily. On good pasture, horses may be pastured well into the fall, and some will flourish mainly on pasture and just a handful of oats once a day to keep them coming to the barn and obedient to your wishes. Horses revert to a seminatural state very quickly if allowed to go unsupervised, and this daily trip to the barn for even a small ration of oats keeps them reminded that they are not doing simply whatever they want, but that they are still under your control.

One thing that is bad in pasture is marshy or wet ground. Boggy pastures are poor ground whereon to keep a horse, not only from the standpoint that the hores's feet will be constantly wet and may soften to too great an extent, but also because mosquitoes live and breed in wet and boggy areas, and mosquitoes carry *encephalitis* or *sleeping sickness*. Though this disease is not carried by all mosquitoes, should an infected mosquito bite your horse, the sickness that will follow the bite is difficult, and sometimes, impossible to cure. Another bad risk attached to pasturing in boggy areas is that of strains and sprains to leg muscles and tendons. It is very easy for a horse to strain and sprain his legs when pastured in marshy areas. Pasture should be level or rolling, with few rocks, and should be fairly dry.

Now, what about clipping and/or blanketing your horse? Many people who ride to the hounds or who ride cross-country in the winter, clip their horses in a pattern, removing any hair that does not serve a purpose, either to protect parts of the horse's body or to provide warmth to specified places. All horses will grow a winter coat, some thicker than others, but all winter coats are hard to dry when they are soaked with sweat after a hard day in the huntfield or on the trail. Clipping the horse removes this coat and permits the shorter hair and the skin to dry quickly, thus lessening the chances of the horse catching cold by standing around with a wet coat. However, if the horse is clipped, he must wear a blanket when not working in order to protect him, since his coat has been shaved off. Horses that have been clipped should be blanketed both in the stable and in the field, as they have no other way of keeping warm. A regular blanket with a liner is fine for the stable, and a New Zealand rug is best for the pasture. New Zealand rugs are thick blankets made especially for providing warmth when a clipped horse is at pasture, however, they need to be properly adjusted as they have leg straps, and they must not be tight enough to bind, yet must be snug enough so that the blanket does not flip up over the flanks, or shift around on the body.

While one often thinks of blanketing a horse, or sees a horse already in a blanket or rug, one does not often stop to think about how it is done, or how the blanket should fit when properly placed on a horse. For those of you just starting out with horses allow me to explain how to properly blanket and unblanket a horse. While the process is anything but complicated, a correct procedure for doing so should be followed. The horse is, by nature, a panicky and nervous animal, and many a young horse has been started on the road to shying by a careless blanketing job. To begin with, the blanket should be folded in half, from back to front and again from side to side. This gives the blanket a quartered effect and lessens the amount of material that will be flapping about when you go to place it on the horse. All straps and tapes should be held neatly on one side so that they do not dangle about and get in the way. To blanket the horse you should take the quarter folded blanket and standing on the near side of the horse, place it across the center of his back, opening the side to side folds. The blanket will now be folded only in half from front to back, and will be hanging down on both sides of him. You should now unfold the front half toward the horse's withers. The blanket will now be fully open and will, no doubt, ride too high against the animals neck. This is proper, for you should now pull the blanket back toward the horse's hindquarters until it is in the proper position for buckling about him. The object in this is to ensure that the hair lies flat and smooth under the blanket and is not pulled the wrong way or against the direction of growth. The tapes or straps will now be lying across the horse's back and should be buckled around him, as though you were girthing up a saddle for a ride. The blanket should fit so that the chest straps, while keeping the blanket in place, do not bind or rub against the chest or windpipe. If the blanket is too far back on the body and you cannot buckle the chest straps, do not pull it front, but remove the blanket and start over. Belly straps, too, should hold the blanket snugly in place, but should not bind or pinch. The hind leg straps of the New Zealand rug should not cut or pinch the thighs, and some horses may take time to get used to the feel of them.

Now, let us suppose that you have time to spend with your horse each day, other than just the time needed for morning feed and evening feed. Let us assume that you will be doing some daily riding. Your daily schedule might appear somewhat like this. Feed, grooming, ride — A.M. Ride, feed — P.M. But, what happens to the horse between A.M. ride and P.M. ride? Many large stables, especially ones who teach the art of riding and of horsemastership, include something called *quarter grooming* or simply *quartering*. This is not a full grooming, but a quick points check, so to speak, to see that the horse is comfortable between rides or feedings. A daily routine in a large stable may appear as follows: The groom that has been appointed to a particular horse comes to the stable before his own breakfast, waters, then feeds his horse, and picks up any droppings done during the night. Or, if the horse is confined to a tie stall, he cleans out the front area of the stall before the horse is fed to provide a clean place for the horse to stand while eating; he waters the horse, feeds him, and then proceeds to clean out the rest of the stall while the horse is eating. (While it is best to have the horse out of the stall while it is being cleaned, many training stables cannot take the time to do so due to crowded schedules, and therefore, the pupils must muck out while the horse is eating). When the horse has finished eating, he is groomed and his stable blanket is put back on to keep him clean until time for his exercise or ride. In some stables it may also be required that his tail be wrapped to keep it neat after grooming. Now, the pupil, or groom, will rake, sweep, or hose down the stable yard, depending upon its construction, and then he may go for his own breakfast. After breakfast and a change of clothes to the required attire, the pupil will return to the stable for the lesson or ride. After the ride comes the quartering. The horse is stripped of saddle and bridle and returned to his stall. There he is quickly brushed with the dandy brush, his feet are checked for stones, etc., he is reblanketed, his water is freshened, and he is given a bit of hay. Then he is allowed to relax until the afternoon ride. Meanwhile his groom cleans tack. After the afternoon ride he is again quartered, then an hour or two later he is fed his supper and his stall is freshened for the night. All droppings are removed at each quartering and then again before the stable is closed for the night when he is again given fresh water.

While this is a very strict routine and is often seen in only those stables that expect to turn out professional horsemen, it can be modified for greater efficiency in your own stable. By having a routine and by sticking to it, your horse will be better cared for, and you will find that your own work will be done better and in less time. Try it for a few weeks, and see if it makes a difference in your stable appearance, as well as that of your horse and your equipment.

FIRST AID KIT

Blueing
Several gauze 2″ x 2″ and 4″ x 4″ pads
Absorbent cotton in sheet form
Cotton balls
Q-tips
Vaseline
Liniment
Rolled guaze
Adhesive tape
Tweezers
Scissors (one pair straight, one pair curved)
Boric acid
Iodine
Four clean, white leg wraps
Rectal thermometer
Cold packs
Clean sponges

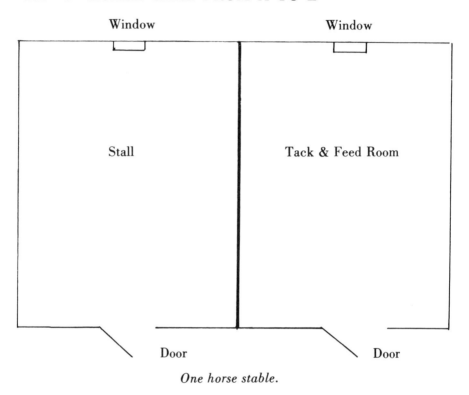

One horse stable.

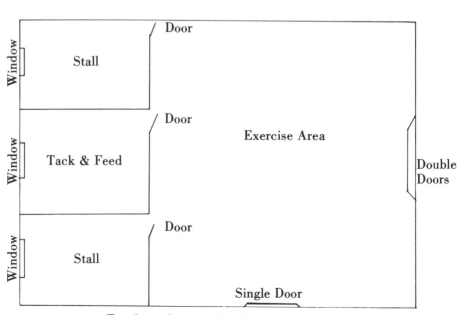

Two horse barn with indoor exercise area.

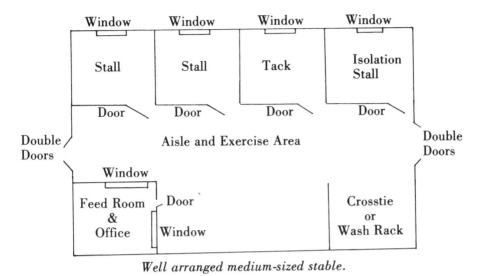

Well arranged medium-sized stable.

Four horse barn—back to back stalls.

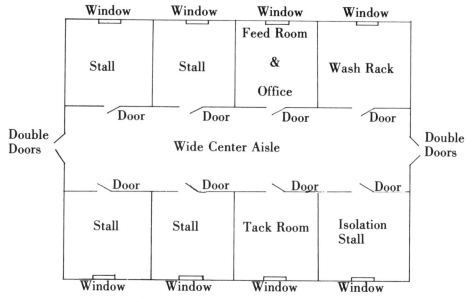

Large stable–racing or show type.

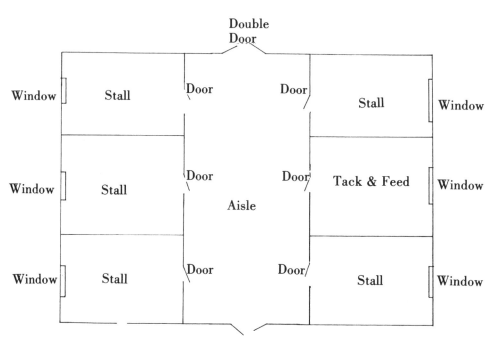

Good arrangement for boarding stable.

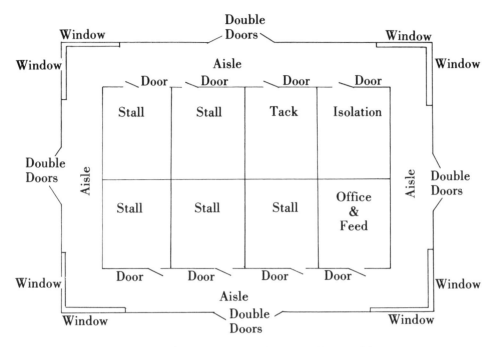

Stable set up for maximum efficiency–show stable type.

11
BITS AND PIECES

Pastures should all be fenced with the best possible material that you can afford. Wooden fencing may be of post and rail, the post being of locust wood, which is resistant to insects and rotting, and coated with creosote to further prevent decomposition of the wood. Or, the wooden fence may be of post and board and painted white for a clean, neat appearance. If your fencing is made of posts and wire, then the wire should be regular or heavy gauge fence wire and should be electrified. Wire fences for horses should be two-strand and should never be barbed wire. Do not let anyone tell you that barbed wire is all right for horses, and that once caught in the barbs will be a good lesson for the horse. Barbed wire does terrible damage to a horse and once caught in the wire, may necessitate his being put to sleep. Fences should be sturdy and well maintained. Broken or weak fencing is an invitation to trouble, and leaving broken fencing hanging from the posts is courting disaster.

Livestock fencing in the square pattern should be not used around horses, as it is too easy for them to slip a leg through a wire opening and then damage it while trying to pull it back out. Too, the heels of the shoes have a tendency to get caught in the wire, and a fence-trapped horse will nearly always panic and do damage to himself.

All property that is used for horses, whether it is used for pasturing, training, or riding, should be posted to hunters and trespassers. Extreme caution should be taken while riding during hunting season, as many hunters disregard the *no hunting* signs and you could be shot at by mistake while riding. Patrol your

222

Excellent example of post and rail fence.

Broken rails not repaired and left hanging from the posts are an open invitation to disaster.

property and advise your local game warden of trespassers and/or hunters if your property is posted and the signs go unheeded or ignored.

Having adequate shade in your pasture is another thing that should be considered for your horse's comfort and well being. Horses, just like humans, are prone to heatstroke and sunstroke, and pasturing horses in the summer without any shade is not only asking for trouble, but is cruel as well. A horse must have a place where he can get relief from the sun. If there are no trees to provide shade for him then a field shed should be built for him. This is a three-sided barnlike structure with no doors that he can go into to escape, not only heat, but also rain.

Innoculation against tetanus, influenza, and encephalitis should be included in each and every stable for each and every horse. It is often too late to do anything once the horse has contracted one of the above diseases. A yearly injection takes little time, and the cost is minimal when weighed against the cost of the horse's life.

12
IN CONCLUSION

Though a large animal, the horse is a delicate one and needs constant and specialized care if he is to develop into his full potential and remain in the best of health and fitness. In order to fully serve his master, the horse needs patience, the best of care, and understanding. Even the most intelligent horse is slow-witted when compared with man, and even with others in the animal kingdom, and he can only rely upon instinct rather than knowing what is right for him and what is wrong; what is good for him and what is bad. It is up to his master to know what to feed him, how to feed, and how much to feed. His master needs to know how to care for his feet, since he is confined, and nature can no longer care for them for him. It is up to his master to keep him warm when cold, cool when the weather is hot, and to see him through sickness and injury to the best of his ability.

The horse is nearly totally dependent on man for his survival, and though many horses could fend for themselves in the wild if turned loose, there are many that would not be able to sustain themselves, as they have been under man's care for so long that they have lost their natural abilities for self-preservation.

If you are going to care for a horse, own a horse, and spend both time and money on having a horse, then do the best you possibly can for that horse, for he is dependent upon you, his master, and you alone, for the kind of life he is to lead.

INDEX